W9-BIS-534

'A groundbreaking book that redefines what it means to be in a relationship.' **John Gray, PhD., bestselling author of** *Men Are from Mars, Women Are from Venus*

'Chock-full of tips, questionnaires, and case studies, this is a solidly researched and intriguing approach to the perennial trials of looking for love in all the right places and improving existing relationships.' *Publishers Weekly*

'A practical, enjoyable guide to forming rewarding romantic relationships.' *Kirkus Reviews*

'Amir Levine and Rachel Heller have written a very smart book: It is clear, easy to read and insightful. It's a valuable tool whether you are just entering a relationship with a new partner or – as in my case – even after you've been married twenty-one years, and had thought you knew everything about your spouse.' *Scientific American*

'Anyone who has been plagued by that age-old question – "What is his deal?" – could benefit from a crash course in attachment theory.' *Elle*

Attached

Are you Anxious, Avoidant or Secure?
How the science of adult attachment
can help you find – and keep – love

DR AMIR LEVINE

AND

RACHEL HELLER

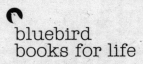

bluebird
books for life

First published 2010 by Penguin US

First published in the UK 2011 by Rodale

This paperback edition published 2019 by Bluebird
an imprint of Pan Macmillan
The Smithson, 6 Briset Street, London EC1M 5NR
EU representative: Macmillan Publishers Ireland Ltd, 1st Floor,
The Liffey Trust Centre, 117–126 Sheriff Street Upper,
Dublin 1, D01 YC43
Associated companies throughout the world
www.panmacmillan.com

ISBN 978-1-5290-3217-8

Neither the publisher nor the authors are engaged in rendering professional advice
or services to the individual reader. The ideas, procedures, and suggestions contained in this
book are not intended as a substitute for consulting with your physician. All matters regarding
your health require medical supervision. Neither the authors nor the publisher shall be liable
or responsible for any loss or damage allegedly arising from any information or suggestion
in this book. While the authors have made every effort to provide accurate telephone numbers
and Internet addresses at the time of publication, neither the publisher nor the authors
assume any responsibility for errors, or for changes that occur after publication.

Pan Macmillan does not have any control over, or any responsibility for,
any author or third-party websites referred to in or on this book.

27

A CIP catalogue record for this book is available from the British Library.

Book design by Amanda Dewey
Printed and bound by CPI Group (UK) Ltd, Croydon, CR0 4YY

Visit **www.panmacmillan.com** to read more about all our books
and to buy them. You will also find features, author interviews and
news of any author events, and you can sign up for e-newsletters
so that you're always first to hear about our new releases.

CONTENTS

PART TWO
The Three Attachment Styles in Everyday Life

PART THREE
When Attachment Styles Clash

PART FOUR
The Secure Way—Sharpening Your Relationship Skills

AUTHOR'S NOTE

In this book we have distilled years of adult romantic attachment research into a practical guide for the reader who wishes to find a good relationship or improve his or her existing one. Attachment theory is a vast and complex field of research that pertains to child development and parenting as well as to romantic relationships. In this book we limit ourselves to romantic attachment and romantic relationships.

In writing this book we set out to transform complex academic ideas into a useful practical resource for everyday life. We refer to several researchers along the way, but inevitably we could not mention many others. We are forever indebted to the wonderful work of countless creative minds in this field, and we regret that we were not able to mention them all.

FOREWORD

It is with great excitement that we write this foreword for the new edition of *Attached*. A lot has changed since it was first published almost ten years ago. Today there is a much greater awareness for the need for close attachments and dependency throughout the lifespan and of the three main attachment styles – Secure, Anxious, and Avoidant. In fact, these terms have become widely known and are now part of mainstream language, often cited in traditional and social media. Countless readers have conveyed to us that they've experienced *Attached* as a true revelation, a turning point in their lives. Many of them expressed a profound relief to discover that their needs for closeness are valid; a biological fact they can embrace. In the responses we've received, readers would often exclaim: 'This should be required reading for anyone who wants to be in a relationship', 'Life changing', 'An eye opener', 'I wish I read this years ago, it would have saved me so much grief'. Knowing about the attachment styles empowers people to harness their biology to work for them rather than against them. It provides a totally new take on why you feel a certain way in a relationship, and also, how you could handle these feeling better and feel happier and more satisfied in your close bonds.

When we first started toying with the idea of writing

Attached, the social climate was very different. Many of the ideas popularized at the time, and that are to a large degree still popular today, purported the concept that dependency is to be discouraged (re: co-dependency) while self-sufficiency is to be congratulated and encouraged. These ideas contradict some basic principles of how our social brain is wired – and specifically that we are programmed to create strong close connections and to rely on others for our emotional wellbeing. These ideas were in such stark contrast to common beliefs at the time that it raised a concern: How can we make these arguments convincing enough to help people see through these common misconceptions? Now, almost ten years later, although the idea that dependency is a fault or flaw continues to prevail in our society, we feel that the tide is starting to turn.

However, in retrospect, tackling large issues such as dependency and self-sufficiency proved to be a relatively easy task compared to that of creating a practical psychological tool based on research data involving the different attachment styles. Writing *Attached* meant creating everyday life solutions from a mountain of scattered pieces of data. When we began this task we were not fully aware of the huge undertaking this would be. We scoured piles of research papers that spanned several decades, each providing piecemeal information about how the attachment styles affect our everyday life. There wasn't an orchestrated manner in which you could easily glean a unified protocol to improve close relationships. Quite the contrary, we labored for several years to take in the multitude of findings and create a cohesive, practical application that readers could use to improve their close relationships. This turned out to be a challenging balancing act that required adhering carefully to the research data, while finding the practical relevance in those data without overreaching our bounds.

Translating the attachment styles to a tool people can use in everyday life enabled us to make a bold practical leap – that not only do we have to be able to assess our own attachment style, but we should also become proficient in determining the attachment styles of others to help us navigate close relationships better. This led us to create the first ever instrument to assess the attachment style of others (see pages 49-74). Devising this tool allowed readers to better assess and understand peoples' insecure or secure approach to life and helped them learn how to better align themselves with other people's beliefs, expectations and ideas of closeness. Deciphering others attachment styles is a new tool to navigate close relationships in order to achieve greater security in all stages of relationships – dating, ongoing relationships, or even in making sense of past ones.

Perhaps because of these new ideas that were put to the fore, *Attached* was received as a revelation by readers from all walks of life. But what is for us probably most rewarding, is that its content resonates with people from vastly different cultures across the globe. The book has been translated into over eighteen languages and it seems that the message and ideas of attachment hold true whether you live in a small village in Peru, in a highrise in Tokyo or Manchester – as well as across genders, sexual orientations and race.

One issue some readers took with *Attached* is the lack of examples of LGBT relationships in the book. In truth, though we regret not adding more examples, because the language of attachment is so universal, one can easily change the gender of the person in the examples provided in the book and still stay true to the core message. This is because attachment is a language we all speak, one that is rooted in the very essence of how our emotional brains are wired.

We now invite you to turn the page and begin a voyage of discovery of what it means to be secure in a relationship. It has transformed our lives, as well at the lives of countless readers who we have heard from over the years. We hope it will make a positive impact on your life too.

Amir Levine and Rachel Heller
May 2019

The New Science of
Adult Attachment

1.

Decoding Relationship Behavior

- *Only two weeks into dating this guy and already I'm making myself miserable worrying that he doesn't find me attractive enough and obsessing about whether or not he's going to call! I know that once again I'll manage to turn all my fears about not being good enough into a self-fulfilling prophecy and ruin yet another chance at a relationship!*
- *What's wrong with me? I'm a smart, good-looking guy with a successful career. I have a lot to offer. I've dated some terrific women, but inevitably, after a few weeks I lose interest and start to feel trapped. It shouldn't be this hard to find someone I'm compatible with.*
- *I've been married to my husband for years and yet feel completely alone. He was never one to discuss his emotions or talk about the relationship, but things have gone from bad to worse. He stays at work late almost every weeknight and on*

weekends he's either at the golf course with friends or watching the sports channel on TV. There's just nothing to keep us together. Maybe I'd be better off alone.

Each of these problems is deeply painful, touching upon the innermost core of people's lives. And yet no one explanation or solution fits the bill. Each case seems unique and personal; each stems from an endless number of possible root causes. Deciphering them would require a deep acquaintance with all the people involved. Past history, previous relationships, and personality type are just a few of the avenues that a therapist would need to pursue. This, at least, is what we, as clinicians in the field of mental health, were taught and believed, until we made a new discovery—one that provided a straightforward explanation for *all* three problems described above and many more. The story of this discovery, and what came after it, is what this book is about.

IS LOVE ENOUGH?

A few years ago, our close friend Tamara started dating someone new:

I first noticed Greg at a cocktail party at a friend's house. He was unbelievably good-looking, and I found the fact that I caught his eye very flattering. A few days later we went out for dinner with some other people, and I couldn't resist the glimmer of excitement in his eyes when he looked at me. But what I found most enticing were his words and an implicit promise of togetherness that he conveyed. The promise of not being alone. He said things like "Tamara, you don't have to be home all by yourself, you can come and work over at my place," "You can call me any time you like." There was comfort in these statements: The comfort of belonging to someone, of not being alone in the world. If I'd only listened carefully, I could have easily heard another message that was incongruent with this promise, a message that made it clear that Greg feared getting too close and was uncomfortable with commitment. Several times he'd mentioned that he'd never had a stable relationship—that for some reason he always grew tired of his girlfriends and felt the need to move on.

Though I could identify these issues as potentially problematic, at the time I didn't know how to correctly gauge their implications. All I had to guide me was the common belief that many of us grow up with: The belief that love conquers all. And so I let love conquer me. Nothing was more important to me than being with him. Yet at the same time the other messages persisted about his inability to commit. I shrugged them off, confident that with me, things would be different. Of course, I was wrong. As we got closer, his messages got more erratic and everything started to fall apart; he began telling me that he was too busy to meet on this night or that. Sometimes he'd claim that his entire work week looked "crazy" and would ask if we could just meet on the weekend. I'd agree, but inside I had a sinking feeling something was wrong, but what?

From then on I was always anxious. I was preoccupied with his whereabouts and became hypersensitive to anything that could possibly imply that he wanted to break up. But while Greg's behavior presented me with ample evidence of his dissatisfaction, he interspersed pushing me away with just enough affection and apologies to keep me from breaking up with him.

After a while, the ups and downs started to take a toll and I could no longer control my emotions. I didn't know how to act, and despite my better judgment, I'd avoid making plans with friends in case he called. I completely lost interest in everything else that was important to me. Before long the relationship couldn't withstand the strain and everything soon came to a screeching halt.

As friends, we were happy at first to see Tamara meet someone new that she was excited about, but as the relationship unfolded, we became increasingly concerned over her growing preoccupation with Greg. Her vitality gave way to anxiousness and insecurity. Most of the time she was either waiting for a call from Greg or too worried and preoccupied about the relationship to enjoy spending time with us as she had done in the past. It became apparent that her work was also suffering, and she expressed some concern that she may lose her job. We had always considered Tamara to be an extremely well-rounded, resilient person, and we were starting to wonder if we were mistaken about her strength. Although Tamara could point out Greg's history of being unable to maintain a serious relationship and his unpredictability, and even acknowledged that she would probably be happier without him, she was not able to muster the strength to leave.

As experienced mental-health professionals, we had a hard time accepting that a sophisticated, intelligent woman like Tamara had so derailed from her usual self. Why was such a successful woman acting in such a helpless way? Why would somebody whom we've known to be so adaptive to most of life's challenges become powerless in this one? The other end of the equation was equally puzzling. Why would Greg send out such mixed messages, although it was clear, even to us, that he *did* love her? There were many possible complex psychological answers to these questions, but a surprisingly simple yet far-reaching insight into the situation came from an unexpected source.

FROM THE THERAPEUTIC NURSERY TO A PRACTICAL SCIENCE OF ADULT LOVE

At about the same time that Tamara was dating Greg, Amir was working part-time in the Therapeutic Nursery at Columbia University. Here, he used attachment-guided therapy to help mothers create a more secure bond with their children. The powerful effect that attachment-guided treatment had on the relationship between mother and child encouraged Amir to deepen his knowledge of attachment theory. This eventually led him to fascinating reading material: research findings first made by Cindy Hazan and Phillip Shaver indicated that adults show patterns of attachment to their romantic partners similar to the patterns of attachment of children with their parents. As he read more about adult attachment, Amir began to notice attachment behavior in adults all around him. He realized that this kind of insight could have astounding implications for everyday life and could help many people in their romantic relationships.

The first thing Amir did, once he realized the far-reaching implications of attachment theory for adult relationships, was to call his longtime friend Rachel. He described to her how effectively attachment theory explained the range of behaviors in adult relationships, and asked her to help him transform the academic studies and scientific data he'd been reading into practical guide-lines and advice that people could use to actually change the course of their lives. And that's how this book came to be.

THE SECURE, THE ANXIOUS, AND THE AVOIDANT

Adult attachment designates three main "attachment styles," or manners in which people perceive and respond to intimacy in romantic relationships, which parallel those found in children: Secure, Anxious, and Avoidant. Basically, *secure* people feel comfortable with intimacy and are usually warm and loving; *anxious* people crave intimacy, are often preoccupied with their relationships, and tend to worry about their partner's ability to love them back; *avoidant* people equate intimacy with a loss of independence and constantly try to minimize closeness. In addition, people with each of these attachment styles differ in:

- their view of intimacy and togetherness
- the way they deal with conflict
- their attitude toward sex
- their ability to communicate their wishes and needs
- their expectations from their partner and the relationship

All people in our society, whether they have just started dating someone or have been married for forty years, fall into one of these categories, or, more rarely, into a combination of the latter two (anxious and avoidant). Just over 50 percent are secure, around 20 percent are anxious, 25 percent are avoidant, and the remaining

3 to 5 percent fall into the fourth, less common category (combination anxious and avoidant).

Adult attachment research has produced hundreds of scientific papers and dozens of books that carefully delineate the way in which adults behave in close romantic ties. These studies have confirmed, many times over, the existence of these attachment styles in adults in a wide range of countries and cultures.

Understanding attachment styles is an easy and reliable way to understand and predict people's behavior in any romantic situation. In fact, one of the main messages of this theory is that in romantic situations, we are programmed to act in a *predetermined* manner.

Where Do Attachment Styles Come From?

•

Initially it was assumed that adult attachment styles were primarily a product of your upbringing. Thus, it was hypothesized that your current attachment style is determined by the way in which you were cared for as a baby: If your parents were sensitive, available, and responsive, you should have a secure attachment style; if they were inconsistently responsive, you should develop an anxious attachment style; and if they were distant, rigid, and unresponsive, you should develop an avoidant attachment style. Today, however, we know that attachment styles in adulthood are influenced by a variety of factors, one of which is the way our parents cared for us, but other factors also come into play, including our life experiences. For more, see chapter 7.

TAMARA AND GREG: A FRESH PERSPECTIVE

We revisited our friend Tamara's story, and saw it in an entirely new light now. Attachment research contained a prototype of Greg—who had an avoidant attachment style—accurate down to the last detail. It summarized how he thought, behaved, and reacted to the world. It predicted his distancing, his finding fault in Tamara, his initiating fights that set back any progress in their relationship, and his enormous difficulty in saying "I love you." Intriguingly, the research findings explained that though he wanted to be close to her, he felt compelled to push her away—not because he wasn't "into her" or because he thought "she's not good enough" (as Tamara had concluded). On the contrary, he pushed her away because he felt the closeness and intimacy increasing.

As it also turned out, Tamara wasn't unique either. The theory explained her behaviors, thoughts, and reactions, typical for someone with an anxious attachment style, with surprising precision as well. It foresaw her increasing clinginess in the face of his distancing; it predicted her inability to concentrate at work, her constant thoughts about the relationship, and her oversensitivity to everything Greg did. It also predicted that even though she decided to break up with him, she could never muster up the courage to do so. It showed why, against her better judgment and the advice of close friends, she would do almost anything to try to be close to him. Most important, this theory revealed why Tamara and Greg found it so hard to get along even though they did indeed love each other. They spoke two different languages and exacerbated each other's natural tendencies—hers to seek physical and emotional closeness and his to prefer independence and shy away from intimacy. The accuracy with which the theory described the pair was uncanny. It was as though the researchers had been privy to the couple's most intimate moments and personal thoughts. Psychological approaches can be somewhat vague, leaving plenty of room for interpretation, but this theory managed to provide precise, evidence-based insight into a seemingly one-of-a-kind relationship.

Although it's not impossible for someone to change his or her attachment style—on average, one in four people do so over a four-year period—most people are unaware of the issue, so these changes happen without their ever knowing they have occurred (or why). Wouldn't it be great, we thought, if we could help people have some measure of control over these life-altering shifts? What a difference it would make if they could consciously work toward becoming more secure in their attachment styles instead of letting life sway them every which way!

Learning about these three attachment styles was a true eye-opener for us; we discovered that adult attachment behavior was everywhere. We were able to view our own romantic behaviors and those of people around us in a fresh new light. By assigning attachment styles to patients, colleagues, and friends, we could interpret their relationships differently and gain much more clarity. Their behavior no longer seemed baffling and complex, but rather predictable under the circumstances.

EVOLUTIONARY TIES

Attachment theory is based on the assertion that the need to be in a close relationship is embedded in our genes. It was John Bowlby's stroke of genius that brought him to the realization that we've been programmed by evolution to single out a few specific individuals in our lives and make them precious to us. We've been bred to be dependent on a significant other. The need starts in the womb and ends when we die. Bowlby proposed that throughout evolution, genetic selection favored people who became attached because it provided a survival advantage. In prehistoric times, people who relied only on themselves and had no one to protect them were more likely to end up as prey. More often than not, those who were with somebody who deeply cared about them survived to pass on to their offspring the preference to form intimate bonds. In fact, the need to be near someone special is so important that the brain has a biological mechanism specifically responsible for creating and regulating our connection with our attachment figures (parents, children, and romantic partners). This mechanism, called the *attachment system*, consists of emotions and behaviors that ensure that we remain safe and protected by staying close to our loved ones. The mechanism explains why a child parted from his or her mother becomes frantic, searches wildly, or cries uncontrollably until he or she reestablishes contact with her. These reactions are coined *protest behavior*, and we all still exhibit them as grown-ups. In prehistoric times, being close to a partner was a matter of life and death, and our attachment system developed to treat such proximity as an absolute necessity.

Imagine hearing news of a plane crash in the Atlantic on the evening your partner is flying from New York to London. That sinking feeling in the pit of your stomach and the accompanying hysteria you'd feel would be your attachment system at work. Your frantic calls to the airport would be your protest behavior.

An extremely important aspect of evolution is heterogeneity. Humans are a very heterogeneous species, varying greatly in appearance, attitudes, and behaviors. This accounts to a great extent for our abundance and for our ability to fit into almost any ecological niche on earth. If we were all identical, then any single environmental challenge would have the potential to wipe us all out. Our variability improves the chances that a segment of the population that is unique in some way might survive when others wouldn't. Attachment style is no different from any other human characteristic. Although we all have a basic need to form close bonds, the *way* we create them varies. In a very dangerous environment, it would be less advantageous to invest time and energy in just one person because he or she would not likely be around for too long; it would make more sense to get less attached and move on (and hence, the avoidant attachment style). Another option in a harsh environment is to act in the opposite manner and be intensely persistent and hypervigilant about staying close to your attachment figure (hence, the anxious attachment style). In a more peaceful setting, the intimate bonds formed by investing greatly in a particular individual would yield greater benefits for both the individual and his or her offspring (hence, the secure attachment style).

True, in modern society, we are not hunted by predators as our ancestors were, but in evolutionary terms we're only a fraction of a second away from the old scheme of things. Our emotional brain was handed down to us by Homo sapiens who lived in a completely different era, and it is their lifestyle and the dangers they encountered that our emotions were designed to address. Our feelings and behaviors in relationships today are not very different from those of our early ancestors.

PROTEST BEHAVIOR IN THE DIGITAL AGE

Armed with our new insights about the implications of attachment styles in everyday life, we started to perceive people's actions very differently. Behaviors that we used to attribute to someone's personality traits, or that we had previously labeled as exaggerated, could now be understood with clarity and precision through the lens of attachment. Our findings shed a new light on the difficulty Tamara experienced in letting go of a boyfriend like Greg who made her miserable. It did not necessarily come from weakness. It originated, instead, from a basic instinct to maintain contact with an attachment figure at all costs and was amplified greatly by an anxious attachment style.

For Tamara, the need to remain with Greg was triggered by the very slightest feeling of danger—danger that her lover was out of reach, unresponsive, or in trouble. Letting go in these situations would be insane in evolutionary terms. Using protest behavior, such as calling several times or trying to make him feel jealous, made perfect sense when seen in this light.

What we really liked about attachment theory was that it was formulated on the basis of the population at large. Unlike many other psychological frameworks that were created based on couples who come to therapy, this one drew its lessons from everyone—

those who have happy relationships and those who don't, those who never get treatment and those who actively seek it. It allowed us to learn not only what goes "wrong" in relationships but also what goes "right," and it allowed us to find and highlight a whole group of people who are barely mentioned in most relationship books. What's more, the theory does not label behaviors as healthy or unhealthy. None of the attachment styles is in itself seen as "pathological." On the contrary, romantic behaviors that had previously been seen as odd or misguided now seemed understandable, predictable, even expected. You stay with someone although he's not sure he loves you? Understandable. You say you want to leave and a few minutes later change your mind and decide that you desperately want to stay? Understandable too.

But are such behaviors effective or worthwhile? That's a different story. People with a secure attachment style know how to communicate their own expectations and respond to their partner's needs effectively *without* having to resort to protest behavior. For the rest of us, understanding is only the beginning.

FROM THEORY TO PRACTICE— DEVELOPING SPECIFIC ATTACHMENT- BASED INTERVENTIONS

By understanding that people vary greatly in their need for intimacy and closeness, and that these differences create clashes, adult attachment findings offered us a new way of looking at romantic relationships. But while the research made it easy to *understand* romantic liaisons better, how can we make a difference in them? The theory held the promise of improving people's intimate bonds, but its translation from the laboratory to an accessible guide—that people can apply to their own lives—didn't exist. Believing that here lies a key to guiding people toward better relationships, we set out to learn as much as we could about the three attachment styles and the ways they interacted in everyday situations.

We started interviewing people from all walks of life. We interviewed colleagues and patients, as well as laypeople of different backgrounds and ages. We wrote summaries of the relationship histories and romantic experiences they shared with us. We conducted observations of couples in action. We assessed their attachment styles by analyzing their comments, attitudes, and behaviors and at times offered specific attachment-based interventions. We developed a technique that allowed people to determine—in a relatively short time—someone else's attachment style. We taught people how they could use their attachment instincts rather than fight them, in order to not only evade unhappy relationships but also uncover the hidden "pearls" worth cultivating—and it worked!

We discovered that unlike other relationship interventions that focus mostly either on singles or on existing couples, adult attachment is an overarching theory of romantic affiliation that allows for the development of useful applications for people in *all* stages of their romantic life. There are specific applications for people who are dating, those in early stages of relationships, and those who are in long-term ones, for people going through a breakup or those who are grieving the loss of a loved one. The common thread is that adult attachment can be put to powerful use in all of these situations and can help guide people throughout their lives to better relationships.

PUTTING INSIGHTS INTO ACTION

After some time, attachment-related lingo became second nature to the people around us. We'd listen to them during a therapy session or at dinner saying, "I can't go out with him, he's clearly avoidant," or "You know me, I'm anxious. A short fling is the last thing I need." To think that until recently they weren't even aware of the three attachment styles!

Tamara, of course, learned everything there was to know about attachment theory and about the new discoveries we'd made—she brought the subject up in nearly every conversation we held. She finally had summoned the strength to break off her loose ties with Greg. Shortly afterward, she began dating again with a vengeance. Equipped with her newly acquired attachment knowledge, Tamara was able to elegantly dodge potential suitors with an avoidant attachment style, who she now knew were not right for her. People whom she would have spent days agonizing over in the past—analyzing what they were thinking, whether they would call or whether they were serious about her—fell by the wayside effortlessly. Instead Tamara's thoughts were focused on assessing whether the new people she met had the capacity to be close and loving in the way that she wanted them to be.

After some time Tamara met Tom, a clearly secure man, and their relationship developed so smoothly she barely discussed it. It wasn't that she didn't want to share intimate details with us, it was that she had found a secure base and there were just no crises or dramas to discuss. Most of our conversations now revolved around the fun things they did, their plans for the future, or her career, which was in full swing again.

GOING FORWARD

This book is the product of our translation of attachment research into action. We hope that you, like our many friends, colleagues, and patients, will use it to make better decisions in your personal life. In the following chapters, you'll learn more about each of the three adult attachment styles and about the ways in which they determine your behavior and attitudes in romantic situations. Past failures will be seen in a new light, and your motives—as well as the motives of others—will become clearer. You'll learn what your needs are and who you should be with in order to be happy in a relationship. If you are already in a relationship with a partner who has an attachment style that conflicts with your own, you'll gain insight into why you both think and act as you do and learn strategies to improve your satisfaction level. In either case, you'll start to experience change—change for the better, of course.

2.

Dependency Is Not a Bad Word

A few years ago, on a TV reality show that features couples who race against each other around the world and perform challenging tasks, Karen and Tim were the show's dream couple: beautiful, sexy, smart, and successful. In the face of the various challenges they encountered, intimate details about their relationship emerged: Karen wanted to get married but Tim was reluctant. He valued his independence and she wanted to get closer. At certain high-pressure moments during the race and often after an argument, Karen needed Tim to hold her hand. Tim was hesitant to do so; it felt too close, and besides, he didn't want to succumb to her every whim.

By the last show Tim and Karen were leading the race. They almost won the big cash prize, but at the finish line they were beaten. When they were interviewed for the season finale, they were asked if in retrospect they'd do anything differently. Karen said: "I think we lost because I was too needy. Looking back I see that my behavior was a bit much. Many times I needed Tim to hold my hand during the race. I don't know why it was so important to me. But I've learned a lesson from that and I've decided that I don't need to be that way anymore. Why did I need to hold his hand so much? That was silly. I should have just kept my cool without needing this gesture from him." Tim, for his part, said very little: "The race in no way resembled real life. It was the most intense experience I have ever had. During the race we didn't even have time to be angry with each other. We just dashed from one task to the next."

Both Karen and Tim neglected to mention an important fact: Tim got cold feet before a joint bungee-jump challenge and almost quit the race. Despite Karen's encouragement and reassurance that she too would be jumping with him, he just wouldn't do it. It reached the point that he took off all his gear and started walking away. Finally, he mustered the courage to take the challenge after all. Because of that particular hesitation they lost their lead.

Adult attachment theory teaches us that Karen's basic assumption, that she can and should control her emotional needs and soothe herself in the face of stress, is simply wrong. She assumed the problem was that she is too needy. Research findings support the exact opposite. Getting attached means that our brain becomes wired to seek the support of our partner by ensuring the partner's psychological and physical proximity. If our partner fails to reassure us, we are programmed to continue our attempts to achieve closeness until the partner does. If Karen and Tim understood this, she would not feel ashamed of needing to hold his hand during the stress of a nationally televised race. For his part, Tim would have known that the simple gesture of holding Karen's hand could give them the extra edge they needed to win. Indeed, if he knew that by responding to her need early on, he would have had to devote less time to "putting out fires" caused by her compounded distress later—he might have been inclined to hold her hand when he noticed that she was starting to get anxious, instead of waiting until she demanded it. What's more, if Tim was able to accept Karen's support more readily, he would probably have bungee jumped sooner.

Attachment principles teach us that most people are only as needy as their unmet needs. When their emotional needs are met, and the earlier the better, they usually turn their attention outward. This is sometimes referred to in attachment literature as the "dependency paradox": The more effectively dependent people are on one another, the more independent and daring they become. Karen and Tim were unaware of how to best use their emotional bond to their advantage in the race.

WE'VE COME A LONG WAY (BUT NOT FAR ENOUGH)

Karen's self-blaming view of herself as too needy and Tim's obliviousness to his attachment role are not surprising and not really their fault. After all, we live in a culture that seems to scorn basic needs for intimacy, closeness, and especially dependency, while exalting independence. We tend to accept this attitude as truth—to our detriment.

The erroneous belief that all people should be emotionally self-sufficient is not new. Not too long ago in Western society people believed that children would be happier if they were left to their own devices and taught to soothe themselves. Then attachment theory came along and turned these attitudes—at least toward children—around. In the 1940s experts warned that "coddling" would result in needy and insecure children who would become emotionally unhealthy and maladjusted adults. Parents were told not to lavish too much attention on their infants, to allow them to cry for hours and to train them to eat on a strict schedule. Children in hospitals were isolated from their parents and could only be visited through a glass window. Social workers would remove children from their homes and place them in foster care at the slightest sign of trouble.

The common belief was that a proper distance should be maintained between parents and their children, and that physical affection should be doled out sparingly. In *Psychological Care of Infant and Child*, a popular parenting book in the 1920s, John Broadus Watson warned against the dangers of "too much mother love" and dedicated the book *"to the first mother who brings up a happy child."* Such a child would be an autonomous, fearless, self-reliant, adaptable, problem-solving being who does not cry unless physically hurt, is absorbed in work and play, and has no great attachments to any place or person.

Before the groundbreaking work of Mary Ainsworth and John Bowlby, the founders of attachment theory in the fifties and sixties, psychologists had no appreciation of the importance of the bond between parent and child. A child's attachment to her mother was seen as a by-product of the fact that she offered food and sustenance; the child learned to associate her mother with nourishment and sought her proximity as a result. Bowlby, however, observed that even infants who had all of their nutritional needs taken care of but lacked an attachment figure (such as infants raised in institutions or displaced during the Second World War) failed to develop normally. They showed stunted physical, intellectual, emotional, and social development. Ainsworth's and Bowlby's studies made it clear that the connection between infant and caretaker was as essential for the child's survival as food and water.

ATTACHMENT NEEDS: THEY'RE NOT JUST FOR CHILDREN

Bowlby always claimed that attachment is an integral part of human behavior throughout the *entire* lifespan. Then Mary Main discovered that adults, too, can be divided into attachment categories according to the way in which they recall their early relationship with their caregivers, which, in turn, influences their parental behavior. Cindy Hazan and Phillip Shaver, independently of Mary Main's work, found that adults have distinct attachment styles in romantic settings as well. They first discovered this by publishing a "love quiz" in the *Rocky Mountain News*, asking volunteers to mark the one statement out of three that best described their feelings and attitudes in relationships. The three statements corresponded to the three attachment styles and read as follows:

- I find it relatively easy to get close to others and am comfortable depending on them and having them depend on me. I don't often worry about being abandoned or about someone getting too close to me. (Measure of the secure attachment style)

- I am somewhat uncomfortable being close to others; I find it difficult to trust them completely, difficult to allow myself to depend on them. I am nervous when anyone gets too close, and often, love partners want me to be more intimate than I feel comfortable being. (Measure of the avoidant attachment style)

- I find that others are reluctant to get as close as I would like. I often worry that my partner doesn't really love me or won't want to stay with me. I want to merge completely with another person and this desire sometimes scares people away. (Measure of the anxious attachment style)

Remarkably, the results showed a similar distribution of attachment styles in adults as that found in infants: Here too most respondents fell under the "secure" category and the remaining subjects were divided between anxious and avoidant. The researchers also found that each style corresponded to very different and unique beliefs and attitudes about themselves, their partners, their relationships, and intimacy in general.

Further studies by Hazan and Shaver and others corroborated these findings. It appears that as Bowlby speculated, attachment continues to play a major role throughout our entire lifespan. The difference is that adults are capable of a higher level of abstraction, so our need for the other person's continuous physical presence can at times be temporarily replaced by the knowledge that the person is available to us psychologically and emotionally. But the bottom line is that the need for intimate connection and the reassurance of our partner's availability continues to play an important role throughout our lives.

Unfortunately, just as the importance of the parent-child bond was disregarded in the past, today the significance of adult attachment goes unappreciated. Among adults, the prevailing notion is still that too much dependence in a relationship is a bad thing.

THE CODEPENDENCY MYTH

The codependency movement and other currently popular self-help approaches portray relationships in a way that is remarkably similar to the views held in the first half of the twentieth century about the child-parent bond (remember the "happy child" who is free of unnecessary attachments?). Today's experts offer advice that goes something like this: Your happiness is something that should come from within and should not be dependent on your lover or mate. Your well-being is not their responsibility, and theirs is not yours. Each person needs to look after himself or herself. In addition, you should learn not to allow your inner peace to be disturbed by the person you are closest to. If your partner acts in a way that undermines your sense of security, you should be able to distance yourself from the situation emotionally, "keep the focus on yourself," and stay on an even keel. If you can't do that, there might be something wrong with you. You might be too enmeshed with the other person, or "codependent," and you must learn to set better "boundaries."

The basic premise underlying this point of view is that the ideal relationship is one between two self-sufficient people who unite in a mature, respectful way while maintaining clear boundaries. If you develop a strong dependency on your partner, you are deficient in some way and are advised to work on yourself to become more "differentiated" and develop a "greater sense of self." The worst possible scenario is that you will end up *needing* your partner, which is equated with "addiction" to him or her, and addiction, we all know, is a dangerous prospect.

While the teachings of the codependency movement remain immensely helpful in dealing with family members who suffer from substance abuse (as was the initial intention), they can be misleading and even damaging when applied indiscriminately to all relationships. Karen, whom we met earlier in the televised race, has been influenced by these schools of thought. But biology tells a very different story.

THE BIOLOGICAL TRUTH

Numerous studies show that once we become attached to someone, the two of us form one physiological unit. Our partner regulates our blood pressure, our heart rate, our breathing, and the levels of hormones in our blood. We are no longer separate entities. The emphasis on differentiation that is held by most of today's popular psychology approaches to adult relationships does not hold water from a biological perspective. Dependency is a fact; it is not a choice or a preference.

A study conducted by James Coan is particularly illuminating to that effect: Dr. James Coan is the director of the Affective Neuroscience Laboratory at the University of Virginia. He investigates the mechanisms through which close social relationships and broader social networks regulate our emotional responses. In this particular study, which he conducted in collaboration with Richard Davidson and Hillary Schaefer, he used functional MRI technology to scan the brains of married women. While these women were being scanned, Dr. Coan and his colleagues simulated a stressful situation by telling them that they were about to receive a very mild electric shock.

Normally, under stressful conditions the hypothalamus becomes activated. And indeed this is what happened in the experiment to the women when they were alone awaiting the shock—their hypothalamus lit up. Next, they tested the women who were holding a stranger's hand while they waited. This time the scans showed somewhat reduced activity in the hypothalamus. And when the hand that the women held was their husband's? The dip was much more dramatic—their stress was barely detectable. Furthermore, the women who benefited most from spousal hand-holding were those who reported the highest marital satisfaction—but we'll get back to this point later.

The study demonstrates that when two people form an intimate relationship, they regulate each other's psychological and emotional well-being. Their physical proximity and availability influence the stress response. How can we be expected to maintain a high level of differentiation between ourselves and our partners if our basic biology is influenced by them to such an extent?

It seems that Karen from our example instinctively understood the healing effect of holding her partner's hand under stressful conditions. Unfortunately, she later gave in to common misconceptions and viewed her instinct as a weakness, something to be ashamed of.

THE "DEPENDENCY PARADOX"

Well before brain imaging technology was developed, John Bowlby understood that our need for someone to share our lives with is part of our genetic makeup and has nothing to do with how much we love ourselves or how fulfilled we feel on our own. He discovered that once we choose someone special, powerful and often uncontrollable forces come into play. New patterns of behavior kick in *regardless* of how independent we are and *despite* our conscious wills. Once we choose a partner, there is no question about whether dependency exists or not. *It always does.* An elegant coexistence that does not include uncomfortable feelings of vulnerability and fear of loss sounds good but is not our biology. What proved through evolution to have a strong survival advantage is a human couple becoming one physiological unit, which means that if she's reacting, then I'm reacting, or if he's upset, that also makes me unsettled. He or she is part of me, and I will do anything to save him or her; having such a vested interest in the well-being of another person translates into a very important survival advantage for both parties.

Despite variations in the way people with different attachment styles learn to deal with these powerful forces—the secure and anxious types embrace them and the avoidants tend to suppress them—all three attachment styles are programmed to connect with a special someone. In fact, chapter 6 describes a series of experiments that demonstrate that avoidants have attachment needs but actively suppress them.

· · ·

Does this mean that in order to be happy in a relationship we need to be joined with our partner at the hip or give up other aspects of our life such as our careers or friends? Paradoxically, the opposite is true! It turns out that the ability to step into the world on our own often stems from the knowledge that there is someone beside us whom we can count on—this is the "dependency paradox." The logic of this paradox is hard to follow at first. How can we act more independent by being thoroughly dependent on someone else? If we had to describe the basic premise of adult attachment in one sentence, it would be: If you want to take the road to independence and happiness, find the right person to depend on and travel down it with that person. Once you understand this, you've grasped the essence of attachment theory. To illustrate this principle, let's take another look at childhood, where attachment starts. While adult and childhood attachment styles are not one and the same, nothing better demonstrates the idea we're conveying than what is known in the field as the strange situation test.

THE STRANGE SITUATION TEST

Sarah and her twelve-month-old daughter, Kimmy, enter a room full of toys. A friendly young research assistant is waiting in the room and exchanges a few words with them. Kimmy starts to explore this newfound toy heaven—she crawls around, picks up toys, throws them to the ground, and checks whether they rattle, roll, or light up, while glancing at her mom from time to time.

Then Kimmy's mother is instructed to leave the room; she gets up and quietly walks out. The minute Kimmy realizes what has happened she becomes distraught. She crawls over to the door as quickly as she can, sobbing. She calls out to her mother and bangs on the door. The research assistant tries to interest Kimmy in a box full of colorful building blocks, but this only makes Kimmy more agitated and she throws one of the blocks in the research assistant's face.

When her mother returns to the room after a short while, Kimmy rushes toward her on all fours and raises her arms to be held. The two embrace and Sarah calmly reassures her daughter. Kimmy hugs her mom tight and stops sobbing. Once she is at ease again, Kimmy's interest in the toys reawakens and she resumes her play.

The experiment Sarah and Kimmy participated in is probably the most important study in the field of attachment theory—referred to as the *strange situation test* (the version described here is an abbreviated version of the test). Mary Ainsworth was fascinated by the way in which children's exploratory drive—their ability to play and learn—could be aroused or stifled by their mother's presence or departure.

She found that having an attachment figure in the room was enough to allow a child to go out into a previously unknown environment and explore with confidence. This presence is known as a *secure base*. It is the knowledge that you are backed by someone who is supportive and whom you can rely on with 100 percent certainty and turn to in times of need. A secure base is a prerequisite for a child's ability to explore, develop, and learn.

A SECURE BASE FOR GROWN-UPS

As adults we don't play with toys anymore, but we do have to go out into the world and deal with novel situations and difficult challenges. We want to be highly functional at work, at ease and inspired in our hobbies, and compassionate enough to care for our children and partners. If we feel secure, like the infant in the strange situation test when her mother is present, the world is at our feet. We can take risks, be creative, and pursue our dreams. And if we lack that sense of security? If we are unsure whether the person closest to us, our romantic partner, truly believes in us and supports us and will be there for us in times of need, we'll find it much harder to maintain focus and engage in life. As in the strange situation test, when our partners are thoroughly dependable and make us feel safe, and especially if they know how to reassure us during the hard times, we can turn our attention to all the other aspects of life that make our existence meaningful.

Brooke Feeney, the director of the Carnegie Mellon University Relationship Lab, illustrates how a secure base works in adult relationships. Dr. Feeney is particularly interested in studying the way in which partners get and give support to each other and the factors that determine the quality of that support. In one of her studies, Dr. Feeney asked couples to discuss their personal goals and exploratory opportunities with one another in the lab. When participants felt that their goals were supported by their partner, they reported an increase in self-esteem and an elevated mood after the discussion. They also rated higher the likelihood of achieving their goals after the discussion than before it. Participants who felt that their partner was more intrusive and/or less supportive, on the other hand, were less open to discussing their goals, did not confidently examine ways for achieving those goals, and tended to downgrade their goals during the course of the discussion.

Back to Karen and Tim, our reality-TV-show couple: In many ways, their experience is a close adult equivalent to the strange situation test for children. Just as Karen needed Tim's hand for encouragement and Tim gathered strength from Karen's reassurance, Kimmy wanted her mother's presence. Karen engaged in protest behavior (not agreeing to continue until he held her hand), just as Kimmy had done when she called out for her absent mother. Both needed the reassurance of their attachment figures before they could focus on other tasks. Only once their secure base was restored could they go back to other activities.

FINDING THE RIGHT PERSON TO DEPEND ON

The question is, what happens when the person we rely on most—and in fact depend on emotionally and physically—doesn't fulfill his or her attachment role? After all, our brain assigns our partner the task of being our secure base, the person we use as an emotional anchor and a safe haven, the one we turn to in time of need. We are programmed to seek their emotional availability. But what if they aren't consistently available? In the Coan MRI experiment, we saw that physical contact with a spouse can help reduce anxiety in a stressful situation, and we also learned that those who reported the highest satisfaction levels in their relationship benefited most from spousal support.

Other experiments have produced even more far-reaching results. Brian Baker, a psychiatrist and researcher at the University of Toronto, studies psychiatric aspects of heart disease and hypertension and, in particular, the way in which marital discord and job strain affect blood pressure. In one of his studies, Dr. Baker found that if you have a mild form of high blood pressure, being in a satisfying marriage is good for you; spending time in the presence of your partner actually benefits you by lowering your blood pressure to healthier levels. If, on the other hand, you are not satisfied with your marriage, contact with your partner will actually raise your blood pressure, which will remain elevated as long as you are in physical proximity! The implications of this study are profound: When our partner is unable to meet our basic attachment needs, we experience a chronic sense of disquiet and tension that leaves us more exposed to various ailments. Not only is our emotional well-being sacrificed when we are in a romantic partnership with someone who doesn't provide a secure base, but so is our physical health.

It seems, then, that our partners powerfully affect our ability to thrive in the world. There is no way around that. Not only do they influence how we *feel* about ourselves but also the degree to which we *believe* in ourselves and whether we will attempt to achieve our hopes and dreams. Having a partner who fulfills our intrinsic attachment needs and feels comfortable acting as a secure base and safe haven can help us remain emotionally and physically healthier and live longer. Having a partner who is inconsistently available or supportive can be a truly demoralizing and debilitating experience that can literally stunt our growth and stymie our health. The rest of the book is about how to go about finding a partner who can become your secure base, becoming that kind of partner yourself, and helping your existing partner take on this life-altering role.

USING THIS BOOK

How can this book guide you in looking for love in all the right places and improving your existing relationships?

After the introduction, we invite you to "roll up your sleeves" and get straight to business by determining your own attachment style. This will allow you to home in on your unique relationship "DNA" or attachment style. Next you'll learn how to identify the attachment styles of those around you. These are key chapters, the first steps in understanding *your* specific needs in relationships and who will be able (or unable) to meet those needs. We'll guide you through this process step-by-step and then give you a chance to practice your new skills.

The next part discusses each attachment style in more detail. You'll start to get a better feel for the inner workings of each style. You may experience these chapters as a true revelation as they allow you to see your own romantic experiences and the experiences of people around you in a fresh new light.

Part three comes with a big warning sign attached. You'll learn the emotional price of connecting with someone who has drastically different intimacy needs from your own. We describe the specific problems of the anxious-avoidant trap and advise you on the cost of remaining in such a relationship. If you are already in such a bond and want to make it work, this part will guide you through the process. By uncovering the specific needs and vulnerabilities of each attachment style (your own and your partner's), and following tips and specific interventions that are tailored to the anxious-avoidant connection, you will be able to bring the relationship to a more secure place. Should you decide to leave, we discuss the pitfalls you'll encounter that may stop you from going through with it and offer some useful pointers on how to survive the pain of a breakup.

Finally, we tap into the mind-set of people with a secure attachment style. We reveal a method for getting your message across effectively to your date or partner. Using this skill will not only convey your needs clearly and from a place of strength and dignity, but it will also provide valuable information about your partner. The quality of his or her response will speak volumes. We also explore the five strategies used by people with a secure attachment style to resolve conflict, and offer a workshop through which you can practice these techniques, so that the next time a conflict comes along, you'll be better prepared. These chapters are a lifeline for those of you who have an anxious or avoidant attachment style—they coach you on how to keep a relationship healthy and fulfilling. Even if you are secure, you may learn a few new tricks that will ultimately lead to an increase in your overall satisfaction level in relationships. These are universal skills that help secure people navigate the world around them more smoothly.

We hope that learning about the powerful force of attachment in your relationships and ways in which to harness it will make a significant difference in your life, as it has in ours.

PART ONE

Your Relationship Toolkit—
Deciphering Attachment Styles

3.

Step One:
What Is My Attachment Style?

The first step toward applying attachment theory to *your* life is to get to know yourself and those around you from an attachment perspective. In the next chapter, we'll walk you through the process of determining your partner or prospective partner's attachment style based on various clues. But let's begin by assessing the person you know best—yourself.

WHICH ATTACHMENT STYLE AM I?

Following is a questionnaire designed to measure your attachment style—the way you relate to others in the context of intimate relationships. This questionnaire is based on the Experience in Close Relationship (ECR) questionnaire. The ECR was first published in 1998 by Kelly Brennan, Catherine Clark, and Phillip Shaver, the same Shaver who published the original "love quiz" with Cindy Hazan. The ECR allowed for specific short questions that targeted particular aspects of adult attachment based on two main categories: anxiety in the relationship and avoidance. Later, Chris Fraley from the University of Illinois, together with Niels Waller and Kelly Brennan, revised the questionnaire to create the ECR-R. We present a modified version that we think works best in everyday life.

Attachment styles are stable but plastic. Knowing your specific attachment profile will help you understand yourself better and guide you in your interactions with others. Ideally this will result in more happiness in your relationships. (For a fully validated adult attachment questionnaire, you can log on to Dr. Chris Fraley's website at: http://www.web-research-design.net/cgi-bin/crq/crq.pl.)

Check the small box next to each statement that is TRUE for you. (If the answer is untrue, *don't* mark the item at all.)

	TRUE		
	A	B	C
I often worry that my partner will stop loving me.	☐		
I find it easy to be affectionate with my partner.		☐	
I fear that once someone gets to know the real me, s/he won't like who I am.	☐		
I find that I bounce back quickly after a breakup. It's weird how I can just put someone out of my mind.			☐
When I'm not involved in a relationship, I feel somewhat anxious and incomplete.	☐		
I find it difficult to emotionally support my partner when s/he is feeling down.			☐
When my partner is away, I'm afraid that s/he might become interested in someone else.	☐		

Step One: What Is My Attachment Style?

	TRUE		
	A	B	C
I feel comfortable depending on romantic partners.		☐	
My independence is more important to me than my relationships.			☐
I prefer not to share my innermost feelings with my partner.			☐
When I show my partner how I feel, I'm afraid s/he will not feel the same about me.	☐		
I am generally satisfied with my romantic relationships.		☐	
I don't feel the need to act out much in my romantic relationships.		☐	
I think about my relationships a lot.	☐		
I find it difficult to depend on romantic partners.			☐
I tend to get very quickly attached to a romantic partner.	☐		
I have little difficulty expressing my needs and wants to my partner.		☐	
I sometimes feel angry or annoyed with my partner without knowing why.			☐
I am very sensitive to my partner's moods.	☐		
I believe most people are essentially honest and dependable.		☐	
I prefer casual sex with uncommitted partners to intimate sex with one person.			☐
I'm comfortable sharing my personal thoughts and feelings with my partner.		☐	

Attached

	TRUE		
	A	**B**	**C**
I worry that if my partner leaves me I might never find someone else.	☐		
It makes me nervous when my partner gets too close.			☐
During a conflict, I tend to impulsively do or say things I later regret, rather than be able to reason about things.	☐		
An argument with my partner doesn't usually cause me to question our entire relationship.		☐	
My partners often want me to be more intimate than I feel comfortable being.			☐
I worry that I'm not attractive enough.	☐		
Sometimes people see me as boring because I create little drama in relationships.		☐	
I miss my partner when we're apart, but then when we're together I feel the need to escape.			☐
When I disagree with someone, I feel comfortable expressing my opinions.		☐	
I hate feeling that other people depend on me.			☐
If I notice that someone I'm interested in is checking out other people, I don't let it faze me. I might feel a pang of jealousy, but it's fleeting.		☐	
If I notice that someone I'm interested in is checking out other people, I feel relieved—it means s/he's not looking to make things exclusive.			☐
If I notice that someone I'm interested in is checking out other people, it makes me feel depressed.	☐		
If someone I've been dating begins to act cold and distant, I may wonder what's happened, but I'll know it's probably not about me.		☐	

Step One: What Is My Attachment Style?

	TRUE		
	A	**B**	**C**
If someone I've been dating begins to act cold and distant, I'll probably be indifferent; I might even be relieved.			☐
If someone I've been dating begins to act cold and distant, I'll worry that I've done something wrong.	☐		
If my partner was to break up with me, I'd try my best to show her/him what s/he is missing (a little jealousy can't hurt).	☐		
If someone I've been dating for several months tells me s/he wants to stop seeing me, I'd feel hurt at first, but I'd get over it.		☐	
Sometimes when I get what I want in a relationship, I'm not sure what I want anymore.			☐
I won't have much of a problem staying in touch with my ex (strictly platonic)—after all, we have a lot in common.		☐	

*Adapted from Fraley, Waller, and Brennan's (2000) ECR-R Questionnaire.

Add up all your checked boxes in column A: _____

Add up all your checked boxes in column B: _____

Add up all your checked boxes in column C: _____

Scoring Key

The more statements that you check in a category, the more you will display characteristics of the corresponding attachment style. Category A represents the *anxious* attachment style, Category B represents the *secure* attachment style, and Category C represents the *avoidant* attachment style.

Anxious: You love to be very close to your romantic partners and have the capacity for great intimacy. You often fear, however, that your partner does not wish to be as close as you would like him/her to be. Relationships tend to consume a large part of your emotional energy. You tend to be very sensitive to small fluctuations in your partner's moods and actions, and although your senses are often accurate, you take your partner's behaviors too personally. You experience a lot of negative emotions within the relationship and get easily upset. As a result, you tend to act out and say things you later regret. If the other person provides a lot of security and reassurance, however, you are able to shed much of your preoccupation and feel contented.

Secure: Being warm and loving in a relationship comes naturally to you. You enjoy being intimate without becoming overly worried about your relationships. You take things in stride when it comes to romance and don't get easily upset over relationship matters. You effectively communicate your needs and feelings to your partner and are strong at reading your partner's emotional cues and responding to them. You share your successes and problems with your mate, and are able to be there for him or her in times of need.

Avoidant: It is very important for you to maintain your independence and self-sufficiency and you often prefer autonomy to intimate relationships. Even though you do want to be close to others, you feel uncomfortable with too much closeness and tend to keep your partner at arm's length. You don't spend much time worrying about your romantic relationships or about being rejected. You tend not to open up to your partners and they often complain that you are emotionally distant. In relationships, you are often on high alert for any signs of control or impingement on your territory by your partner.

WHAT IF I'M *STILL* NOT SURE?

When people hear about attachment styles, they often have no difficulty recognizing their own style. Some people tell us right away, "I'm anxious," "I'm definitely avoidant," or "I think I'm secure." Others have a harder time figuring it out. If you scored high on more than one attachment style, you may find it helpful to learn that two dimensions essentially determine attachment styles:

- Your comfort with intimacy and closeness (or the degree to which you try to *avoid* intimacy).
- Your anxiety about your partner's love and attentiveness and your preoccupation with the relationship.

What we find particularly helpful is the way in which Brennan and his colleagues present attachment styles in graphic form, which provides a bird's-eye view of attachment styles that helps you understand how your attachment style relates to those of others. Your location on these two axes determines your attachment style, as the following schematic shows:

THE TWO ATTACHMENT DIMENSIONS

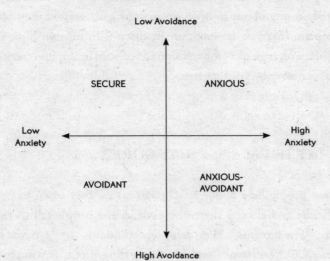

(Based on Brennan, Clark, and Shaver's Two Attachment Dimension Scale)

- If you feel comfortable with intimacy with your romantic partner (i.e., are low on intimacy avoidance) and don't obsess much about the relationship or about your partner's ability to love you back (i.e., are low on relationship anxiety) but coast along with it—you're probably secure.
- If you crave intimacy and closeness (i.e., are low on intimacy avoidance) but have a lot of insecurities about where the relationship is going, and little things your partner does tend to set you off (i.e., are high on relationship anxiety)—you're probably anxious.
- If you feel uncomfortable when things become too close and intimate and value your independence and freedom more than the relationship (i.e., are high on intimacy

avoidance) and don't tend to worry about your partner's feelings or commitment toward you (i.e., are low on relationship anxiety)—you're probably avoidant.

- If you are both uncomfortable with intimacy and very concerned about your partner's availability, you have a rare combination of attachment anxiety and avoidance. Only a small percentage of the population falls into this category and if you are one of them, you can benefit from information on both the anxious and avoidant attachment styles.

Out of the Mouths of Babes

•

Where do these classifications come from? Interestingly enough, they come from watching babies' behavior. Attachment styles were first defined by researchers observing the way babies (usually 9 to 18 months old) behaved during the strange situation test (a reunion with a parent after a stressful separation, described on page 29).

Here's a short description of how attachment styles are defined in children. Some of their responses can also be detected in adults who share the same attachment style.

Anxious: This baby becomes extremely distressed when mommy leaves the room. When her mother returns, she reacts ambivalently—she is happy to see her but angry at the same time. She takes longer to calm down, and even when she does, it is only temporary. A few seconds later, she'll angrily push mommy away, wriggle down, and burst into tears again.

Secure: The secure baby is visibly distressed when mommy leaves the room. When mother returns, he is very happy and eager to greet her. Once in the safety of her presence, he is quick to be reassured, calm down, and resume play activity.

Avoidant: When mommy leaves the room, this baby acts as though nothing has happened. Upon her return, she remains unmoved, ignores her mom, and continues to play indifferently. But this façade doesn't tell the whole story. In fact, inside, baby is neither calm nor collected. Researchers have found that these babies' heart rates are actually just as elevated as other babies who express immense distress, and their cortisol levels—a stress hormone—are high.

4.

Step Two:
Cracking the Code—
What Is My Partner's Style?

Figuring out other people's attachment styles is usually trick-ier than identifying your own. For one, you know yourself best—not just how you behave but also what you feel and think when you are in a relationship. Second, you can take your own quiz to help with the process. When you start dating some-one new, however, you aren't likely to whip out our quiz and start grilling your date about his or her past relationships. Luckily, with-out even knowing it, most people give away almost all the infor-mation you need to determine their attachment style in their natural, day-to-day actions and words.

The trick is to know what to look for, be a keen observer and ardent listener. In attachment studies, researchers bring people to the lab and ask them about their romantic relationships. The at-titudes that people display toward intimacy and closeness and the degree to which they are preoccupied with their relationships determine their attachment style. But from our experience, this information is also readily available outside the lab, if you know what to look for.

Understanding attachment will change the way you perceive new people you meet, but it will also give you surprising insight into your partner if you are already in a relationship.

In dating situations, your thinking will shift from "Does he or she like me?" to "Is this someone I should invest in emotionally? Is he or she capable of giving me what I need?" Going forward with a relationship will become about choices *you* have to make. You'll start asking yourself questions like: "How much is this person capable of intimacy? Is he sending mixed messages or is he genuinely interested in being close?" Using this chapter as a guide, with time and practice you will develop and fine-tune your ability to determine someone's attachment style early on. Keep in mind that when you're excited about someone, your objectivity is compromised and you tend to create a rosy picture of him or her. Anything that doesn't fit into this picture fades into the background. In the initial stages of dating, however, it's important to pay equal attention to *all* messages coming through and address them securely. This will help you determine if the relationship is right for you and ensure it is going in a positive direction.

If you are currently in a relationship, you might already have an idea about your partner's attachment style from what you've read so far, and you can use the tools provided in the following pages to sharpen your skills. Your thinking will shift as well. You'll no longer ask yourself, "Why is she always pushing me away?" Instead you'll say, "It really isn't about me at all—she just doesn't feel comfortable with too much closeness." Uncovering your partner's attachment style will allow you to better understand the particular challenges that you face as a couple—an essential step toward using attachment principles to improve your bond.

QUESTIONNAIRE: DETERMINING YOUR PARTNER'S ATTACHMENT STYLE

Following is a questionnaire designed to help you establish your partner's or date's attachment style.

The questionnaire is divided into three groups. Each describes certain characteristics illustrated with a few examples. *Note that if the characteristic in general is true of your partner, you should score it as true. It is also enough that only one example, and not all, be true of your partner to mark it as true.* After reading each characteristic, decide on the basis of all your interactions and conversations with your partner or date whether it is true of him/her. The truer it is, the higher you should score, based on the following scale:

SCORING KEY
1. Very *untrue* of him or her
2. Moderately true of him or her
3. Very *true* of him or her

Score	Description
1 2 3	**1. Sends mixed signals.** • Seems distant and aloof yet vulnerable at the same time (which you find irresistible). • Sometimes calls a lot and other times not at all. • Says something intimate like "When we move in together . . ."; but later acts as though you don't have a future as a couple.
1 2 3	**2. Values his/her independence greatly**—looks down on dependency and "neediness." • "I need a lot of space." • "My work takes up so much of my time there's no room for anyone serious in my life right now." • "I could never be with someone who isn't completely self-sufficient."
1 2 3	**3. Devalues you** (or previous partners)—even if only jokingly. • Jokes about how lousy you are at reading maps or how "cute" it is that you're roly-poly. • Describes someone s/he was once really interested in but after a couple of dates became turned off by because of some physical feature. • Cheated on a past partner.

Score	Description
1 2 3	**4. Uses distancing strategies—emotional or physical.** • Had a previous partner for six years, but they lived in separate households. • Prefers to go to sleep at home, to use separate blankets, or to sleep in a separate bed. • Prefers taking vacations alone. • Plans are left unclear—when you will meet again, when s/he will move in. • Stays a stride ahead of you when you're walking together.
1 2 3	**5. Emphasizes boundaries in the relationship.** • Makes you feel that "These are MY friends [or family]—keep out!" • Doesn't want to invite you to his/her place, prefers to spend time at yours.
1 2 3	**6. Has an unrealistically romantic view of how a relationship should be.** • Talks longingly about finding that one perfect person one day. • Idealizes a past relationship but is vague about what went wrong. • "I don't know if I'll ever be able to feel again the way I did about my ex."
1 2 3	**7. Mistrustful—fears being taken advantage of by partner.** • Is sure that dates are out to "hitch" him/her into marriage. • Fears partner will take financial advantage of him or her.

Score	Description
1 2 3	**8. Has rigid view of relationships and uncompromising rules** (which you must comply with). • Has a strong preference for a certain "type" of partner: very good-looking or very thin or blond, for example. • Is certain it's best to live in separate houses or not to get married. • Makes sweeping statements like "All women/men want such-and-such" or "After you get married or move in together, they change on you." • Doesn't like talking on the phone even if this is your main way to connect.
1 2 3	**9. During a disagreement, needs to get away or "explodes."** • "You know what, forget it, I don't want to talk about it." • Gets up and walks out in fury.
1 2 3	**10. Doesn't make his/her intentions clear—leaves you guessing as to his/her feelings.** • Stays with you for a long time but doesn't say "I love you." • Talks about going abroad for a year without mentioning where that leaves the two of you.
1 2 3	**11. Has difficulty talking about what's going on between you.** • Makes you feel uncomfortable for asking where the relationship is headed. • When you say something is bothering you, responds "I'm sorry . . ." without further clarification. • Certain topics are off-limits.

(Add the scores for questions 1–11.)

Group A Total Score: _____

GROUP B

Score	Description
1 2 3	**1. Reliable and consistent.** • Phones when s/he says s/he'll phone. • Makes plans in advance and follows through. If can't make it, gives advance notice, apologizes, and specifies an alternative plan. • Doesn't go back on promises. If s/he can't keep promise—explains!
1 2 3	**2. Makes decisions with you** (not unilaterally). • Discusses plans, doesn't like to decide without hearing your opinion first. • Makes plans that take your preferences into account. Doesn't assume s/he knows best.
1 2 3	**3. Flexible view of relationships.** • Isn't looking for a particular type of partner;, e.g., a certain age or appearance. • Is open to different arrangements—like moving in together, or joint versus separate bank accounts. • Doesn't make sweeping statements like "All women/men want such-and-such" or "After you get married or move in together, they change on you."
1 2 3	**4. Communicates relationship issues well.** • Makes you feel comfortable for asking about where the relationship stands or how s/he sees your future together (even if the answer isn't to your liking). • Tells you if something is bothering him or her; doesn't act out or expect you to guess.

Score	Description
1 2 3	**5. Can reach compromise during arguments.** • Does his/her best to understand what is *really* bothering you and to address that issue. • When you have a misunderstanding, is not too busy proving s/he is right to solve the problem.
1 2 3	**6. Not afraid of commitment or dependency.** • Doesn't worry that you are trying to impinge on his/her territory or freedom. • Isn't afraid you or other partners are trying to trap him/her into marriage, get his/her money, etc.
1 2 3	**7. Doesn't view relationship as hard work.** • Doesn't talk about how much compromise and effort a relationship takes. • Is open to starting a new relationship even when circumstances aren't ideal (e.g., when work/studies take up much time).
1 2 3	**8. Closeness creates further closeness** (rather than distancing). • After an emotional or revealing conversation, reassures you and is there for you. Doesn't suddenly get cold feet! • After sleeping together, tells you how much you mean to him/her (not *just* how good the sex was).
1 2 3	**9. Introduces friends and family early on.** • Wants to make you part of his/her circle of friends. Might not initiate your meeting his/her family, but if you ask to meet them or invite him/her to meet yours, will be happy to.
1 2 3	**10. Naturally expresses feelings for you.** • Usually tells you early on how s/he feels about you. • Uses those three words "I love you" generously.

Step Two: What Is My Partner's Style?

Score	Description
1 2 3	**11. Doesn't play games.** • Doesn't leave you guessing or try to make you feel jealous. • Doesn't make calculations such as "I already called twice, now it's your turn" or "You waited an entire day to get back to me, now I'll wait a day too."

(Add the scores for questions 1–11.)

Group B Total Score: _____

GROUP C

Score	Description
1 2 3	**1. Wants a lot of closeness in the relationship.** • Agrees to go on joint vacations, move in together, or spend all your time together early in relationship (although might not initiate it). • Likes a great deal of physical contact (holding hands, caressing, kissing).
1 2 3	**2. Expresses insecurities—worries about rejection.** • Asks a lot of questions about your past partners to assess where s/he stands in comparison. • Tries to see whether you still have feelings for your ex. • Tries hard to please you. • Fears that you'll stop having feelings toward him/her or will lose sexual interest.

Score	Description
1 2 3	**3. Unhappy when not in a relationship.** • You can sense that he or she is desperate to find someone even if he/she doesn't say so. • Sometimes the date feels like an interview for the "future husband/wife" slot.
1 2 3	**4. Plays games to keep your attention/interest.** • Acts distant and uninterested if you haven't called for a few days. • Pretends to be unavailable or busy. • Tries to manipulate certain situations to make you more available/interested in her/him.
1 2 3	**5. Has difficulty explaining what's bothering him/her. Expects you to guess.** • Expects you to pick up from subtle cues that s/he is upset. (If this doesn't work, acts out.)
1 2 3	**6. Acts out—instead of trying to resolve the problem between you.** • Threatens to leave during an argument (but later changes his/her mind). • Doesn't express his/her needs but eventually acts upset about an accumulation of hurts.
1 2 3	**7. Has a hard time *not* making things about himself/herself in the relationship.** • If you have to work late when s/he has a party, interprets it as "You don't want to meet my friends." • If you come home tired and don't want to talk, interprets it as "You don't love me anymore."

Score	Description
1 2 3	**8. Lets you set the tone of the relationship so as not to get hurt.** • You call, s/he calls; you say you have feelings, s/he says s/he has feelings for you (at least at first). Doesn't want to take chances.
1 2 3	**9. Is preoccupied with the relationship.** • At the end of a date, you go home to sleep. S/he goes home to hash out every detail with friends. • When you're not together, calls or texts a lot *or* doesn't call at all and waits for you to call (as a defensive act). • You can tell that s/he thinks about the relationship a lot.
1 2 3	**10. Fears that small acts will ruin the relationship; believes s/he must work hard to keep your interest.** • Says things like "I called you so many times today, I'm afraid you'll get tired of me" or "I really didn't present myself very well to your family, and now your family will hate me."
1 2 3	**11. Suspicious that you may be unfaithful.** • Gets access to your password and checks your e-mail account. • Hypervigilant about your whereabouts. • Goes through your belongings looking for evidence.

(Add the scores for questions 1–11.)

Group C Total Score: _____

SCORING KEY

1. 11–17: Very low. Your partner definitely doesn't have this attachment style.
2. 18–22: Moderate. Your partner shows a tendency toward this attachment style.

3. 23–33: High. Your partner definitely has this attachment style.

As a rule of thumb, the higher the score, the stronger the inclination toward that style. Any score of 23 or above indicates a strong
likelihood of a particular attachment style. If your partner is high
on *two* attachment styles, chances are that those are the avoidant
and anxious ones. Some of the behaviors of these two styles are
outwardly similar (even though they originate from very different
romantic attitudes). In that case, go ahead to the "Golden Rules"
on page 62 to make a better assessment.

Score of 23 or above for group A: It seems that your partner/
date has an avoidant attachment style. This means that you can't
take closeness and intimacy for granted. Someone secure or anxious
has a basic wish to be close; with someone avoidant that basic desire is missing. While they have a need for attachment and love—
they too posses a basic mechanism in the brain to get attached—they
tend to feel suffocated when things get too close. With avoidants,
everyday interactions and conversations, whether they're about
which channel to watch on TV or how to raise the kids, are actually
negotiations for space and independence. You often wind up com-
plying with their wishes—because otherwise they will withdraw.
Research shows that avoidants hardly ever date one another. They
simply lack the glue that keeps things together.

Score of 23 or above for group B: Your partner/date has a
secure attachment style. Such people want to be close; at the same
time they are not overly sensitive to rejection. They are also great
communicators and know how to get their message across in a way
that is straightforward yet not accusing. Once you get close to

someone with this attachment style, you don't have to negotiate intimacy anymore: *It becomes a given.* This frees both of you to enjoy life and grow. They listen to your point of view and try to make things work in a way that will be acceptable to you both. They have an innate understanding of what a romantic partnership means—namely, that your partner's well-being is your own and vice versa. These qualities allow you to be your most authentic self, which research has shown to be one of the most important factors contributing to your overall happiness and well-being.

Score of 23 or above for group C: Your partner/date has an anxious attachment style. This is not necessarily a bad thing as long as you take the trouble to get into his or her mind-set. Someone with an anxious attachment style craves intimacy but is also very sensitive to even the smallest of perceived threats to this closeness. Sometimes they'll interpret your unconscious actions as a threat to the relationship. When this happens, they become flooded with apprehension, but they lack the skills to communicate their distress to you effectively. Instead, they resort to a lot of acting out and drama. This can create a vicious cycle as they become even more sensitive to slights and their distress is compounded. This does sound daunting, but before you call it quits, it is important to know that if you're sensitive and nurturing enough to calm their fears—which is very doable—you will win a greatly loving and devoted partner. Once you are receptive to their basic needs for warmth and security, their sensitivity can become an asset; they'll be very much in tune with your wants and will be helpful and dedicated. What's more, they will also gradually learn how to communicate their fears and emotions better and you will need to second-guess them less and less.

THE GOLDEN RULES FOR DECIPHERING ATTACHMENT STYLES

If you're still in doubt, here are what we call the five Golden Rules to help you home in on his or her attachment style:

1. Determine whether s/he seeks intimacy and closeness.

This is the number-one question to ask yourself about your partner. All other attachment traits and behaviors stem from this one overriding issue. If the answer is no, you can be pretty sure your partner/date has an avoidant attachment style. If the answer is yes, your partner/date has either a secure or anxious style (see chapter 3 to learn more about the two dimensions that determine attachment styles). When trying to answer this question, let go of preconceptions. There is no one type of personality that is avoidant, nor one that is either secure or anxious. He might be cocky and self-assured and still really crave closeness. On the flip side, she might be nerdy and clumsy and still be averse to intimacy. Ask yourself, what does this particular behavior indicate about his or her attitude toward intimacy and closeness? Are they doing or not doing something because they want to minimize intimacy?

Suppose you are dating someone with children from a previous marriage. She might not want to introduce you to them because she is thinking of their well-being and believes it is too early for them to deal with a new man in her life, which is perfectly legitimate. On the other hand, it could be a way for her to keep you at a distance and maintain her separate life. You have to look at the whole picture and see how this behavior fits in. Depending on how much time has passed and how serious the relationship is, does it still seem right for her to be so protective of the kids? What makes sense in the initial stages of the relationship doesn't make sense after two years. Does she introduce you to other family members and close friends? Has she considered your well-being and explained the situation, allowing you to express your feelings about it? If the answer to any of these questions is no, then this is not just about her children's best interests; it is more about keeping you at bay.

2. Assess how preoccupied s/he is with the relationship and how sensitive s/he is to rejection.

Does he get easily hurt by things you say? Is he worried about your future together or about whether you love him enough to stay faithful? Is he very sensitive to details in the relationship that suggest distancing, such as when you make decisions that don't take him into account? If the answer to these questions is yes, it is likely he has an anxious attachment style.

3. Don't rely on one "symptom," look for various signs.

Looking at one behavior, attitude, or belief is not enough to determine your partner's attachment style. That is why there is no *one* characteristic that can establish someone's style but rather a combination of behaviors and attitudes that together create a coherent pattern. It is the whole picture that tells the true story. Not being allowed to meet your partner's kids can be very frustrating, but if she is also able to talk about the subject, listen to your frustration, and find other ways to let you into her life, it doesn't necessarily indicate an inability to be close.

4. Assess his/her reaction to effective communication.

This is probably one of the most important ways to uncover your partner's attachment style: *Don't be afraid to express your needs, thoughts, and feelings to your partner!* (See chapter 11 for more on effective communication.) What often happens when we're dating is that we censor ourselves for different reasons: We don't want to sound too eager or needy or we believe it's too soon to raise a certain topic. However, expressing your needs and true feelings can be a useful litmus test of the other person's capacity to meet your needs. The response, in real time, is usually much more telling than anything he or she could ever reveal of their own accord:

- **If s/he's secure**—s/he'll understand and do what's best to accommodate your needs.
- **If s/he's anxious**—you'll serve as a useful role model. He or she will welcome the opportunity for greater intimacy and start to become more direct and open.
- **If s/he's avoidant**—s/he will feel very uncomfortable with the increased intimacy that your emotional disclosure brings and will respond in one of the following ways:

- "You're too sensitive/demanding/needy."
- "I don't want to talk about it."
- "Stop analyzing everything!"
- "What do you want from me? I didn't do anything wrong."
- He or she will consider your needs on a certain matter only to disregard them again very soon after.
- "Geez, I said I was sorry."

5. Listen and look for what he or she is *not* saying or doing.

What goes unsaid or undone by your partner can be just as informative as what he or she is doing and saying. Trust your gut feeling. Consider these examples:

At midnight on New Year's Eve, Rob kissed his girlfriend and said, "I'm so glad that I'm with you. I hope that this will be the first of many new years for us together." His girlfriend kissed him back but did not reply. Two months later they separated.

During an argument, Pat told her boyfriend, Jim, that it bothered her that they never made plans ahead of time. She felt more comfortable and secure if she had advance notice and a better sense of their plans. Jim didn't answer; he just changed the subject. He continued calling only at the last minute. She mentioned it again, but again he ignored her. Finally Pat gave up on the relationship.

In these cases, what Rob's girlfriend and Jim *didn't* say spoke louder than any words.

CRACKING OTHERS' ATTACHMENT STYLE CHEAT SHEET

Avoidant	Secure	Anxious
Sends mixed signals.	Reliable and consistent.	Wants a lot of closeness in the relationship.
Values his/her independence greatly.	Makes decisions with you.	Expresses insecurities—worries about rejection.
Devalues you (or previous partners).	Flexible view of relationships.	Unhappy when not in a relationship.

Avoidant	Secure	Anxious
Uses distancing strategies—emotional or physical.	Communicates relationship issues well.	Plays games to keep your attention/interest.
Emphasizes boundaries in the relationship.	Can reach compromise during arguments.	Has difficulty explaining what's bothering him/her. Expects you to guess.
Has an unrealistically romantic view of how a relationship should be.	Not afraid of commitment or dependency.	Acts out.
Mistrustful—fears being taken advantage of by partner.	Doesn't view relationship as hard work.	Has a hard time *not* making things about him/herself in the relationship.
Has rigid view of relationships and uncompromising rules.	Closeness creates further closeness.	Lets you set the tone of the relationship.
During a disagreement, needs to get away or "explodes."	Introduces friends and family early on.	Is preoccupied with the relationship.
Doesn't make his/her intentions clear.	Naturally expresses feeling for you.	Fears that small acts will ruin the relationship; believes s/he must work hard to keep your interest.
Has difficulty talking about what's going on between you.	Doesn't play games.	Suspicious that you may be unfaithful.

Golden Rules:

Determine whether s/he seeks intimacy and closeness.

Assess how preoccupied s/he is with the relationship and how sensitive s/he is to rejection.

Don't rely on one "symptom," look for various signs.

Assess his/her reaction to effective communication.

Listen and look for what he or she is *not* saying or doing.

DECIPHERING ATTACHMENT STYLES WORKSHOP

Read the following accounts. Can you identify the attachment style in each case? Cover the answers with a piece of paper if you really want to test yourself, keeping in mind the prevailing traits and Golden Rules we've just outlined (see the chart above).

1. Barry, divorced, 46.

Relationship? I don't want to hear about it now. I am still licking the wounds from my divorce. I want to make up for the time that I was married. I want to feel that women desire me. I want lots of sex. I know I have to be careful, though, because every woman that I go out with immediately starts to fantasize about what kind of father I'll be to her kids and how our last names will sound together. I've been dating someone for almost a year now, her name is Caitlin and she's great in every way. I know she would love for us to become more serious, but it will take me a long time before I'm ready to trust another woman, to commit and love. But even then I know exactly what I *don't* want and what I'm not willing to compromise on. Like what? Well, she'll have to be financially self-sufficient because I already have one woman milking me dry; I have no intention of supporting two! But there are also some other lines that I'm not willing to cross.

Attachment Style: _____

Answer: Avoidant. You might be saying to yourself that the guy just went through a divorce and is bound to be cautious. That may be so, but until we hear evidence to the contrary—he's avoidant. He says that even after he falls in love he will not compromise, that he values his independence, that he's mistrustful. Notice how he even talks about "her kids"? He could be talking about a woman with children from a previous marriage, but it's also possible that even when imagining their *joint* kids, Barry views them as "her kids." The language that he uses creates distance. He's also afraid of being taken advantage of by women who want to tie him down in marriage and of being exploited financially. Consider the first Golden Rule: Determine if s/he seeks intimacy and closeness. You know he doesn't; he talks about wanting to be sought after and a lot of sex but mentions nothing about emotional support or closeness.

2. Bella, single, 24.

Mark and I have been dating for a year and a half. We're very happy together. Don't get me wrong, not everything was perfect from day one. There were several things that bothered me about Mark at first. One example is that when we met, Mark was inexperienced sexually, and to be quite honest, I had to literally coach him in bed. I wasn't going to live the rest of my life sexually frustrated! But that's ancient history. Also, I'm much wilder than he is. Mark is a serious, down-to-earth type of guy; in fact, at first I thought he was too geeky for me to date. But I couldn't have made a better choice—Mark is warm and dependable—qualities that are priceless. I love him to bits.

Attachment Style: _____

Answer: Secure. The clearest and most decisive clue that Bella is secure is the fact that she coached Mark in bed. This is a great example of communicating relationship issues clearly and effectively. She encounters a problem, wants to solve it, and feels confident enough to do so. Were Bella anxious she might blame herself for Mark's deficiencies in bed; she might conclude that he's simply not attracted to her and therefore not making that extra effort to please her. Alternatively, she might grin and bear the situation so as not to harm the relationship. If Bella were avoidant, she wouldn't blame herself, but she might use Mark's incompetence to belittle him, a distancing strategy, and probably wouldn't coach him in the matter-of-fact way that she did. It is also apparent that Bella has flexible views of couplehood. Although Mark did not meet her definition of the "ideal man," she made the mental transition without much hesitation and, more important, is very satisfied with her decision in retrospect. Here too, if she were avoidant, she might make the same compromise, but most likely she would feel cheated for having to make it. Lastly, Bella expresses her feelings for Mark openly and naturally.

3. Janet, single, 23.

I've finally met a great guy, a really great guy. Tim and I have been out together twice and I already feel myself falling in love. It's so hard to find someone I'm compatible with—I'm only attracted to a certain type of man, and then what are the chances he'll also find me attractive? The odds are against me on this one. So now that I've met Tim, I want to make sure I do everything right. I can't afford to make any mistakes. One wrong move and I could jeopardize the entire relationship. I'm waiting for him to set the pace because I don't want to seem too eager. Perhaps a text message would be okay? That might seem laid back and spontaneous, don't you think? Or maybe I'll forward him some funny e-mail as part of a distribution list?

Attachment Style: _____

Answer: Anxious. Janet is typically anxious. She seeks closeness, feels incomplete on her own, and is very preoccupied with the relationship. Granted, on the first few dates people of all attachment styles get excited about the other person and think about them a lot. However, with Janet it goes a step further—she views relationships as rare and fragile and believes that any small, inappropriate act on her part has the capacity to ruin them. Therefore, she turns over in her head every move she makes, countless times, so as not to make a "mistake." She also chooses to let Tim set the tone and pace of the relationship. Last, because she's insecure, she plays games by considering ways of indirectly getting in touch with Tim without putting herself on the line, such as making up a distribution list as an excuse to send him an e-mail.

4. Paul, single, 37.

I just ended my relationship with Amanda. I'm very disappointed, but I know I could never have spent my life with her. We dated for a couple of months and at first I was sure I'd found the woman of my dreams. But different things about her started to bother me. For one thing, I'm convinced she's had cosmetic surgery and that's a real turn-off. Also, she's not that sure of herself, which I find unappealing. And once I stop having feelings toward someone, I can't stay a minute longer. I'll just have to keep searching. I know that the right woman is somewhere out there waiting for me, and no matter how long it takes, we will meet and be together. It's a visceral feeling; I can see her smile and feel her embrace. I know that when we meet I will immediately feel a sense of calm and quietness. No matter how many times I fail, I promise myself that I will continue to look.

Attachment Style: _____

Answer: Avoidant. This one might be confusing. Paul is yearning for the woman of his dreams, so he must be secure or anxious, right? Wrong. His description of an ideal "true love" should raise a red flag. Also, people with different attachment styles tend to explain why they are still alone in a different manner: People who are anxious often feel that there is something wrong with them; secures will have a more realistic view of things, and avoidants often sound like Paul—they attribute their single status to external circumstances, such as not having met the right girl. This is a good opportunity to look beyond what is said to what is *not* said: If you don't get a clear understanding of why this person hasn't met "the one" even though he's dated a great number of women, you should try to read between the lines. There are also hints in the way Paul describes his relationship with Amanda—he was very excited about her, but after they got close, he started noticing little things about her that turned him off. Devaluing your partner when things become too close is very typical of people with an avoidant attachment style and is used as a way to create emotional distance.

5. Logan, single, 34.

I've only dated three people in my life, including Mary. When we met a couple of years ago, I remember Mary was very unsettled by this fact. She kept grilling me about my past relationships, and when she realized I really had told her about all my relationships and was not holding anything back, she looked puzzled and asked if I hadn't felt I was missing out on something. Hadn't I been worried that I was by myself for too long? Or that I wasn't going to find someone? Honestly, the thought that I wouldn't find someone never crossed my mind. Sure, I had my share of disappointments, but I figured that when the time was right it would happen. And it did. I knew I loved Mary almost immediately and told her so. When did she reciprocate? I'm actually not sure, but I knew she was crazy about me even before she told me.

Attachment Style: _____

Answer: Secure. There are several clues here that Logan has a secure attachment style. He is not preoccupied with relationships nor does he fear remaining alone, which rules out an anxious attachment style (although it sounds like his girlfriend, Mary, is anxious for these reasons). The question remains whether Logan has an avoidant or secure style. Several indicators rule out an avoidant style: First, he seems to be very forthcoming with Mary about his past relationships, puts all his cards on the table, and isn't annoyed by her nosiness (and doesn't embellish his romantic history as someone anxious might do). Second, he feels comfortable expressing his feelings for Mary very early on, which is a typically secure trait. If he were avoidant, he'd be more likely to send mixed signals. Also, notice that he doesn't engage in any game playing—he doesn't keep track of when Mary reciprocates; he is simply true to himself and acts in the most genuine manner without letting other considerations rule.

6. Suzanne, single, 33.

This Valentine's Day will mark the beginning of the year when I will find my husband. I'm tired of being alone; I'm sick of coming back to an empty home, going to the movies by myself, having sex with myself or with some stranger. This year I will find someone wonderful who will be mine! In the past, I devoted myself completely to my partners and got badly hurt. I lost faith in finding someone good. But I have to overcome the fear of getting hurt. I'm willing to put myself out there, willing to take a risk and lose myself. I understand that no pain, no gain, and without me opening my heart there is no chance that someone could enter. I will not give in to desperation. I deserve to be happy!

Attachment Style: _____

Answer: Anxious. This is a clear account of someone anxious who's been hurt many times before. She's very absorbed in finding someone. She wants to get out there and find her soul mate, but because she is unfamiliar with attachment principles, she doesn't know who to avoid and who to trust. Suzanne is very different from Paul in example 4. She is not looking for the "ideal" partner. We get an idea of what the matter is and why she hasn't met someone yet—she gets close and then gets hurt, but she continues to yearn for closeness. Paul will not get close until he meets the "right woman." People like Suzanne are one of the reasons we wrote this book. She desperately wants to meet someone, yet she's been burned before and fears rejection. She knows the painful fallout of dating the wrong guy and she's become fearful of that pain almost to the point of giving up. Because she craves intimacy, she feels lonely and incomplete, but she has no clue how to assess potential partners. With knowledge of applied adult attachment, we have seen people like Suzanne learn how to navigate the world of dating, steer clear of avoidants, and land safely in the arms of a nurturing, secure partner.

PART TWO

The Three Attachment Styles
in Everyday Life

Living with a Sixth Sense for Danger: The Anxious Attachment Style

The famous seventeenth-century philosopher Baruch Spinoza said: "All happiness or unhappiness solely depends upon the quality of the object to which we are attached by love." So choose wisely when you are getting involved with someone, because the stakes are high: Your happiness depends on it! We find this to be particularly true for people with anxious attachment style. By being unaware of the attachment system, they risk suffering a great deal in relationships, as can be seen in the example of Amir's colleague Emily.

YOU'RE ONLY AS TROUBLED AS THE RELATIONSHIP YOU'RE IN

When Emily was in her psychiatry residency, she decided she also wanted to become a psychoanalyst. Before starting classes at the psychoanalytic institute, she was required to embark on her own analysis for at least a year, going to therapy four times a week, lying on the couch and talking about whatever came to mind. In the beginning, Emily was doing very well. In fact, she appeared so put together that her analyst thought that she would be done with the analysis within two years max—unheard of, considering that analysis usually lasts at least four to five years.

Then she met David, whom she fell for very quickly. David, an aspiring actor, turned out to be bad news. He gave her mixed signals about wanting to be together, and this really unnerved Emily. It changed her behavior until she appeared to have completely destabilized. We used to run together around the reservoir in Central Park, and she would bring both her work pager and cell phone with her (and in those days cell phones were relatively big and heavy!). She would alternate checking first the one and then the other every few minutes just to see if he had called. At work she would spend hours tracking David's activities on the then-novel Internet, creating a false Internet persona and chatting him up in the chat rooms he frequented. In short, she became obsessed.

Her analyst could not make sense of this horrible transformation in his most promising candidate. From a resilient, together person, Emily began to change into someone with "masochistic borderline personality traits." It now seemed that analysis would take many years.

A SENSITIVE ATTACHMENT SYSTEM

But Emily's was not a case of masochism or borderline personality disorder. It was a simple case of an activated attachment system. People with an anxious attachment style like Emily have a super-sensitive *attachment system*. As we mentioned in previous chapters, the attachment system is the mechanism in our brain responsible for tracking and monitoring the safety and availability of our attachment figures. If you have an anxious attachment style, you possess a unique ability to sense when your relationship is threatened. Even a slight hint that something may be wrong will activate your attachment system, and once it's activated, you are unable to calm down until you get a clear indication from your partner that he or she is truly there for you and that the relationship is safe. People with other attachment styles also get activated, but they don't pick up on subtle details that people with an anxious attachment style do.

To demonstrate how sensitive the attachment system of people with an anxious attachment style is, a study from Chris Fraley's lab at the University of Illinois at Urbana-Champaign—he is the same researcher who designed the ECR-R attachment styles inventory—in collaboration with Paula Niedenthal from Blaise Pascal University in Clermont-Ferrand, France, found a unique way of measuring the vigilance to social cues of the anxious attachment style. They used a "morph movie" technique—a computerized movie in which a face initially displays a specific emotional expression (e.g., anger) and gradually evolves into one displaying a neutral expression. Participants were asked to stop the movie at the frame at which they believed the original emotion had dissipated. They found that people with an anxious attachment style were more likely to perceive the offset of emotion earlier than other people. Also, when the task was reversed—starting with a neutral face and gradually moving to a pronounced expression— more anxious individuals perceived the onset of the emotion earlier. These findings suggest that people with an anxious attachment style are indeed more vigilant to changes in others' emotional expression and can have a higher degree of accuracy and sensitivity to other people's cues. However, this finding comes with a caveat. The study showed that people with an anxious attachment style tend to jump to conclusions very quickly, and when they do, they tend to misinterpret people's emotional state. Only when the experiment was designed in such a way that anxious participants had to wait a little longer—they couldn't react immediately when they spotted a change, but had to wait a little longer—and get more information before making a judgment did they have an advantage over other participants. This is an important lesson for someone with an anxious attachment style: If you just wait a little longer before reacting and jumping to conclusions, you will have an uncanny ability to decipher the world around you and use it to your advantage. But shoot from the hip, and you're all over the place making misjudgments and hurting yourself.

Once activated, they are often consumed with thoughts that have a single purpose: to reestablish closeness with their partner. These thoughts are called *activating strategies*.

Activating strategies are any thoughts or feelings that compel you to get close, physically or emotionally, to your partner. Once he or she responds to you in a way that reestablishes security, you can revert back to your calm, normal self.

Activating Strategies

•

Thoughts and Feelings That Compel You to Seek Closeness with Your Partner

- Thinking about your mate, difficulty concentrating on other things.
- Remembering only their good qualities.
- Putting them on a pedestal: underestimating your talents and abilities and overestimating theirs.
- An anxious feeling that goes away only when you are in contact with them.
- Believing this is your only chance for love, as in:
  - "I'm only compatible with very few people—what are the chances I'll find another person like him/her?"
  - "It takes years to meet someone new; I'll end up alone."
- Believing that even though you're unhappy, you'd better not let go, as in:
  - "If she leaves me, she'll turn into a great partner—for someone else."
  - "He can change."
  - "All couples have problems—we're not special in that regard."

In Emily's case, her attachment system was right on target. During the course of their relationship, she learned that David was watching Internet porn for hours while she was at work and he was supposedly out auditioning. She also found out that he was flirting online with other girls (including her made-up persona) in various chat rooms. But she still had a hard time breaking up with him. She was bombarded by activating strategies similar to those we've outlined above, thinking that he would change, that everyone has problems, and so on. It took over a year before she could muster the courage to sever the tie. During that time and for quite a while after the break, Emily spent her analysis talking mostly about him. Years later, after she married a great guy and went back to being her resilient self, she looks back at the whole experience with bewilderment. She can't believe she wasted her time in therapy examining the deep-seated roots of her "fanatical" behaviors surrounding that relationship. If only she had met a good guy sooner—one who didn't continuously activate her attachment system—she would have spared herself from the unnecessary scrutiny of her "masochistic borderline personality traits."

THE WORKING OF THE ATTACHMENT SYSTEM

For someone who gets attached very quickly and has a very sensitive attachment system, learning how the system functions is invaluable. Many people with anxious attachment style, like Emily, live with a chronically activated attachment system without realizing it. On the following page we illustrate how the attachment system works.

Living with a Sixth Sense for Danger

THE ATTACHMENT SYSTEM:

FINDING YOUR WAY TO THE COMFORT ZONE

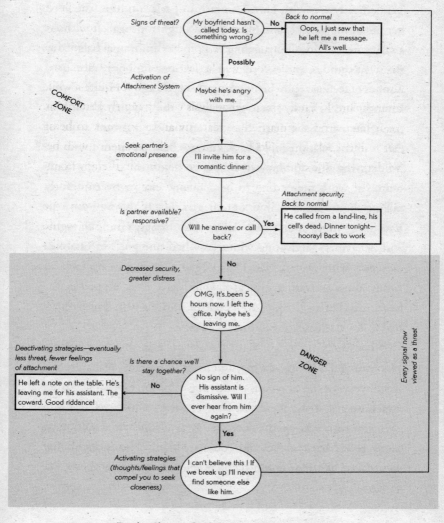

(Based on Shaver and Mikulincer's 2002 integrative model)

While Emily was with David, in terms of relationships, she lived her life in the *danger zone.* She felt like a tightrope walker without a safety net, anxiously struggling to keep her emotional balance as she went through endless cycles of activation, with only rare, brief respites of feeling secure before the cycle began again. Her thoughts, feelings, and behaviors were governed by the fact that David was not truly available to her. She felt an almost constant sense of threat to the relationship. She was always busy trying to minimize it by staying close to him—be it by spending many precious hours online at work pretending to be someone else or by constantly talking about him in analysis or to her friends. In this way, she kept him in her mind at all times. All these seemingly erratic thoughts and behaviors—activating strategies—had one goal: to establish closeness with David. Had David been consistently available to Emily, these activating strategies would have been nipped in the bud instead of escalating out of control, and she would never have had to leave the relationship *comfort zone.*

Now Emily no longer finds herself stuck in the danger zone. Her husband is loving, caring, and most important, available. She is still very aware, however, of the powerful force of an activated attachment system. Were she ever to enter another relationship with someone who wasn't consistently available, she would most likely revert back to her old "obsessed" self. The thought that something like that could happen again sends chills down her spine.

LIVING IN THE COMFORT ZONE: RYAN AND SHAUNA

Ryan and Shauna were coworkers who fell in love. They'd been together for several months when Ryan left that workplace to take a high-paying job with a prestigious firm. For the first time, the couple didn't spend their workdays together anymore. When Ryan went on his first business trip with his new colleagues, he missed Shauna and tried to call her. The call went to voice-mail after two rings. He knew that wasn't right, got really upset, and called again. This time it went directly to voice-mail. He didn't leave a message. He felt hurt that she had pushed the "ignore" button the first time and then turned off her phone completely the second time. He found it hard to concentrate during his business meeting, but he promised himself he wouldn't call her for the rest of his trip. Luckily, an hour later Shauna texted to apologize for not picking up—she hadn't been able to answer because her boss was standing right next to her when he called. He was relieved and called her right back.

Ryan, who has an anxious attachment style, has a sixth sense for attachment-related cues; he is very much in tune with the small details related to his girlfriend's availability: He paid attention to how many times the phone rang before going to voice-mail. He correctly concluded that Shauna hit the "ignore" button and then turned off her phone, cues that might have gone unnoticed by someone with a different attachment style. He was especially sensitive because he was used to having Shauna three offices down from his, and this was his first trip with his new firm.

Fortunately for Ryan, Shauna has a secure attachment style and was able, without much effort, to effectively respond to him, re-establish contact, and calm his attachment system. Unlike Emily, Ryan did not find himself in the relationship danger zone, because his anxieties were met by reassurance.

Notice that if you feel unsettled in a relationship situation, all that is required is a minimal reassurance from your partner—one text message in Shauna's case—to get back on track. But if you don't get that reassurance, your worries about the relationship will quadruple, and it will take a lot more than a simple text to calm your attachment system. This is a very important insight for anyone in a relationship. The more attuned you are to your partner's needs at the early stages—and he or she to yours—the less energy you will need to expend attending to him or her later.

In fact, had Shauna not reacted as she had, Ryan would have continued to find it hard to concentrate at work (activating strategies), and would probably have either acted distant or exploded on the phone (protest behavior) when she eventually did call. All of which would have been very destructive for the relationship.

Protest Behavior—Letting Your Attachment System Get the Best of You

•

Excessive attempts to reestablish contact:
- Calling, texting, or e-mailing many times, waiting for a phone call, loitering by your partner's workplace in hopes of running into him/her.

Withdrawing:

- Sitting silently "engrossed" in the paper, literally turning your back on your partner, not speaking, talking with other people on the phone and ignoring him/her.

Keeping score:

- Paying attention to how long it took them to return your phone call and waiting just as long to return theirs; waiting for them to make the first "make-up" move and acting distant until such time. When Ryan decided not to leave a message for Shauna after she screened his calls, he was keeping score ("If she's not answering my calls, I won't leave her a message").

Acting hostile:

- Rolling your eyes when they speak, looking away, getting up and leaving the room while they're talking (acting hostile can transgress to outright violence at times).

Threatening to leave:

- Making threats—"We're not getting along, I don't think I can do this anymore," "I knew we weren't really right for each other," "I'll be better off without you"—all the while hoping s/he will stop you from leaving.

Manipulations:

- Acting busy or unapproachable. Ignoring phone calls, saying you have plans when you don't.

Making him/her feel jealous:
- Making plans to get together with an ex for lunch, going out with friends to a singles bar, telling your partner about someone who hit on you today.

Protest behavior is any action that tries to reestablish contact with your partner and get their attention. There are many ways that protest behavior can manifest itself, anything that can jolt the other person into noticing you and responding to you.

Protest behavior and activating strategies can cause you to act in ways that are harmful to the relationship. It is very important to learn to recognize them when they happen. (In chapter 8, you'll find the relationship inventory, which is designed to help you identify your protest behaviors and find more constructive ways of handling difficult situations.) These behaviors and strategies can also continue long after your partner is gone. This is part of what heartache is all about—the longing for someone who is no longer available to us when our biological and emotional makeup is programmed to try to win them back. Even if your rational mind knows you shouldn't be with this person, your attachment system doesn't always comply. The process of attachment follows its own course and its own schedule. This means you will continue to think about the other person and will be unable to push them out of your mind for a very long time.

It turns out that people with anxious attachment styles are particularly susceptible to falling into a chronically activated attachment system situation. A study conducted by Omri Gillath,

Silvia Bunge, and Carter Wendelken, together with two promi-nent attachment researchers, Phillip Shaver and Mario Mikulincer, found fascinating evidence for this. Using fMRI technology, they asked twenty women to think about—and then stop thinking about—various relationship scenarios. Intriguingly, they found that when women with an anxious attachment style thought about negative scenarios (conflict, breakup, death of partner), emotion-related areas of the brain became "lit up" to a greater degree than in women with other attachment styles. What's more, they found that regions of the brain associated with emotional regulation, such as the orbitofrontal cortex, were *less* activated than in woman with other attachment styles. In other words, the brains of people with an anxious attachment style react more strongly to thoughts of loss and at the same time under-recruit regions normally used to down-regulate negative emotions. This means that once your attachment system is activated, you will find it much harder to "turn it off" if you have an anxious attachment style.

Understanding the attachment system is crucial for people with an anxious attachment style. Therein lies their chance for a happy, fulfilling relationship.

We've divided our guidance for people with an anxious attach-ment style into two separate routes—the first is for those of you who are unattached. Finding a secure partner in the first place is the best option available for you if you are single. It can work like magic to prevent hardship before it even starts—but going secure might be trickier than you think. The rest of this chapter is dedi-cated to directing singles with an anxious attachment style toward a secure partner, avoiding pitfalls on the way. The second route is for anyone who has an anxious attachment style—both those currently in a relationship and those who are still on the lookout for the right partner. It entails reshaping your attachment working models—basically rethinking your attitudes and beliefs about relationships from an attachment perspective—as a segue toward retooling yourself with more secure relationship skills. Parts Three and Four are dedicated to this second group.

THE SECRET TO FINDING A GOOD RELATIONSHIP IF YOU ARE ANXIOUS

Emily, who you met at the beginning of the chapter, was unaware of attachment science. She didn't know that she had an anxious attachment style. She was also unaware that the man she was obsessed with, David, had an avoidant attachment style. If she had known, she would have understood that being anxious means that she thrives on intimate, supportive relationships that are stable and long-lasting, and that uncertainty and emotional unavailability get her activated and preoccupied, or in a word, miserable. She would also have known that certain people—namely, avoidants—intensify her worries and feelings of inadequacy, while others—secures—pacify them. Emily, like most anxious people, paradoxically often ends up dating people with an avoidant attachment style even though findings in adult attachment make a clear case for people with an anxious style going well with secures. Why is this so? And most important, how can you find happiness and avoid unnecessary heartache?

GRAVITATIONAL PULL?

A number of studies have looked into the question of whether we are attracted to people based on their attachment style or ours. Two researchers in the field of adult attachment, Paula Pietromonaco, of the University of Massachusetts, and Katherine Carnelley, of the University of Southampton in the UK, found that avoidant individuals actually prefer anxiously attached people. Another study, by Jeffry Simpson of the University of Minnesota, showed that anxious women are more likely to date avoidant men. Is it possible, then, that people who guard their independence with ferocity would seek the partners most likely to impinge on their autonomy? Or that people who seek closeness are attracted to people who want to push them away? And if so, why?

Pietromonaco and Carnelley believe that these attachment styles actually complement each other in a way. Each reaffirms the other's beliefs about themselves and about relationships. The avoidants' defensive self-perception that they are strong and independent is confirmed, as is the belief that others want to pull them into more closeness than they are comfortable with. The anxious types find that their perception of wanting more intimacy than their partner can provide is confirmed, as is their anticipation of ultimately being let down by significant others. So, in a way, each style is drawn to reenact a familiar script over and over again.

THE EMOTIONAL ROLLER COASTER

But there's another reason you might be attracted to an avoidant partner if you are anxious. In Emily's case, David's subtle indicators of uncertainty and unavailability made her feel insecure. This is often what happens, even very early in the relationship, if you are anxious and dating an avoidant. Quite soon into the relationship you start to get mixed signals. He (or she) calls, but takes his time about it; he's interested in you, but lets you understand that he's still playing the field. You are left guessing. Every time you get mixed messages, your attachment system is activated and you become preoccupied with the relationship. But then he compliments you or makes a romantic gesture that gets your heart racing, and you tell yourself he's interested after all; you're elated. Unfortunately, the bliss is very short-lived. Quickly the positive messages become mixed once again with ambiguous ones and again you find yourself plunging down that roller coaster. You now live in suspense, anticipating that next small remark or gesture that will reassure you. After living like this for a while, you start to do something interesting. You start to equate the anxiety, the preoccupation, the obsession, and those ever-so-short bursts of joy with love. What you're really doing is equating an activated attachment system with passion.

If you've been at it for a while, you become programmed to get attracted to those very individuals who are least likely to make you happy. Having a perpetually activated attachment system is the opposite of what nature had in mind for us in terms of gratifying love. As we've seen, one of Bowlby and Ainsworth's most important insights is that in order to thrive and grow as human beings, we need a secure base from which to derive strength and comfort. For that to happen, our attachment system must be calm and secure.

Remember, an activated attachment system is *not* passionate love. Next time you date someone and find yourself feeling anxious, insecure, and obsessive—only to feel elated every once in a while—tell yourself this is most likely an activated attachment system and *not love*! True love, in the evolutionary sense, means peace of mind. "Still waters run deep" is a good way of characterizing it.

If You're Anxious, You Shouldn't Be Dating Someone Avoidant Because:

•

You: want closeness and intimacy.

They: want to maintain some distance, emotional and/or physical.

You: are very sensitive to any signs of rejection (vigilant attachment system).

They: send mixed signals that often come across as rejecting.

You: find it hard to tell them directly what you need and what's bothering you (effective communication), and use protest behavior instead.

They: are bad at reading your verbal and nonverbal cues and don't think it's their responsibility to do so.

You: need to be reassured and feel loved.

They: tend to put you down to create distance as a means to deactivate their attachment system.

You: need to know exactly where you stand in the relationship.

They: prefer to keep things fuzzy. Even if your relationship is very serious, some question marks still remain.

THE LAW OF LARGE NUMBERS— WHY YOU ARE MORE LIKELY TO MEET AVOIDANTS WHEN YOU GO OUT ON A DATE

There is one last reason you will probably meet and date a fair share of avoidant people. Consider the following three facts:

- People with an avoidant attachment style tend to end their relationships more frequently. One study found that of individuals who entered a new marriage following a divorce, the avoidant ones were more likely to divorce again. They also suppress loving emotions and therefore "get over" partners very quickly so they can start dating again almost immediately. *Conclusion: Avoidants are in the dating pool more frequently and for longer periods of time.*

- People with a secure attachment style usually don't go through many partners before they find one that they happily settle down with. Once things click, they form a long-lasting, committed relationship. *Conclusion: People with a secure attachment style take a very long time to reappear in the dating pool, if at all.*

- Studies have found that avoidants are unlikely to be in a relationship with other avoidants, because they lack the emotional glue to stay together. In fact, one study that looked at dating couples didn't find even one pair that was avoidant-avoidant. *Conclusion: Avoidants don't date each other; they are more likely to date people with different attachment styles.*

Now let's put the pieces of this puzzle together.

When you meet someone new, the probability that they have an avoidant attachment style is high—much higher than their relative size in the population—25 percent. Not only are they recycled back into the dating pool more quickly, but they are not dating one another (at least not for long), nor are they dating secure people, that much because secures are less available. Who *are* they meeting? That's right: You and other potential partners with an anxious attachment style.

WHAT HAPPENS WHEN YOU DO MEET SOMEONE SECURE?

Let's say you get past the statistical obstacles and do meet someone secure. Do you realize you've stumbled upon a gold mine or do you let it pass you by? Several years ago Rachel tried to set up her neighbor Chloe with her acquaintance Trevor—a real (secure) catch. Trevor, then in medical school, was looking to meet someone new after his girlfriend of ten years left him. He had been with her from the age of 18 to 28. He hadn't wanted to break up even though she was always discontented; finally she left him. He was very sad for a long while but was ready to start dating again. Trevor was very good-looking, had a great sense of humor, and was a superb athlete. He was strong-willed and stable and came from a well-to-do, educated family. All the traits you would want in a partner, right?

Not quite. Chloe met him once and was utterly uninterested. She conceded that he was very handsome and even attractive, but "the spark was missing." At the time, Rachel was dumbfounded. She didn't understand why she was turning him down.

In hindsight, we do understand: If you are anxious, the reverse of what happens when you meet someone avoidant happens when you meet someone secure. The messages that come across from someone secure are very honest, straightforward, and consistent. Secures are not afraid of intimacy and know they are worthy of love. They don't have to beat around the bush or play hard to get. Ambiguous messages are out of the mix, as are tension and suspense. As a result, your attachment system remains relatively calm. Because you are used to equating an activated attachment system with love, you conclude that this can't be "the one" because no bells are going off. You associate a calm attachment system with boredom and indifference. Because of this fallacy you might let the perfect partner pass you by.

Chloe had to go through terrible hardship because she assumed an activated attachment system was a prerequisite for love. Tony, who eventually became her husband, seemed confident and intriguing at first, but he never missed a chance to put her down.

Luckily, both Trevor's and Chloe's stories have happy endings. Trevor did not stay available for long. He quickly found a great partner and they have been together ever since. They traveled around the world, got married, and had a couple of kids. He is a wonderful father and husband. Chloe had a harder time, but after several years of agony with Tony, she got her act together and learned to appreciate the stability and love of a secure partner. She divorced Tony and later met Bruce, who is as loving and caring as Trevor.

Anyone can have a happy ending like that. It's not entirely up to chance. The trick is not to get hooked on the highs and lows and mistake an activated attachment system for passion or love. Don't let emotional unavailability turn you on.

If You're Anxious, You *Should* Be Dating Someone Secure Because:

•

You: want closeness and intimacy.

They: are comfortable with closeness and don't try to push you away.

You: are very sensitive to any signs of rejection (vigilant attachment system).

They: are very consistent and reliable and won't send mixed messages that will upset you. If you become distressed, they know how to reassure you.

You: find it hard to tell them directly what you need and what's bothering you (effective communication), and use protest behavior instead.

They: see your well-being as a top priority and do their best to read your verbal and nonverbal cues.

You: need to be reassured and feel loved.

They: feel comfortable telling you how they feel, very early on, in a consistent manner.

You: need to know exactly where you stand in the relationship.

They: are very stable; they also feel comfortable with commitment.

WHAT HAPPENS WHEN YOU FOLLOW COMMON DATING ADVICE?

Say you decide to follow the advice of many popular relationship books. They offer guidelines to help you "land" a partner, such as: Don't make yourself too available, say you're busy even when you're not, don't call him—wait for him to call you, don't appear to care too much, act mysterious. Presumably, you preserve your dignity and independence in this way and gain your partner's respect. But in fact, what you are doing is behaving in a way that is not true to your genuine needs and feelings. You wave these aside to appear strong and self-sufficient. And indeed, these books and the advice they give *are* right; these behaviors may indeed make you seem more attractive. What they don't mention, because they are unaware of attachment science, is that they will make you seem more attractive to a very particular kind of partner—an avoidant one. Why? Because, in essence, what they are advocating is that you ignore your needs and let the other person determine the amount of closeness/distance in the relationship. The avoidant person can have his/her cake and eat it too, so to speak—s/he can enjoy the thrill and closeness you naturally project when you are together without having to consider your needs for intimacy and togetherness the rest of the time. By being someone you're not, you're allowing another to be with you on his or her own terms and come and go as s/he pleases.

Another problem is that if this type of game playing is only an act for you, it's going to backfire in the long run. First, your avoidant partner will quickly catch on to you—they are good at detecting people who want to impinge on their autonomy. Second, eventually you'll think it's time to let your true colors show. After all, what you really want is to reach a high degree of intimacy, to spend a lot of quality time together, to be able to let down your guard. But you'll find that when you do so, your avoidant partner will suddenly get cold feet and start to disengage. Either way, you lose, because you are attracting *the wrong kind of partner for you.*

A COACHING SESSION FOR THE ANXIOUS ATTACHMENT STYLE ON A DATE

1. Acknowledge and accept your true relationship needs.

Do we recommend that you do all the pursuing, fulfill your partner's every wish, and call incessantly? Definitely not. We suggest a completely different approach. It stems from the understanding that you—given your anxious attachment style—have certain clear needs in a relationship. If those needs are not met, you cannot be truly happy. The key to finding a mate who can fulfill those needs is to first fully acknowledge your need for intimacy, availability, and security in a relationship—and to believe that they are legitimate. They aren't good or bad, they are simply your needs. Don't let people make you feel guilty for acting "needy" or "dependent." Don't be ashamed of feeling incomplete when you're not in a relationship, or for wanting to be close to your partner and to depend on him.

Next, use this knowledge. Start assessing people you date on the basis of their ability to meet those needs. Instead of thinking how you can change *yourself* in order to please your partner, as so many relationship books advise, think: Can this person provide what *I* need in order to be happy?

2. Recognize and rule out avoidant prospects early on.

The second step is to recognize and rule out people with an avoidant attachment style early on. This is where our questionnaire for deciphering the style of others comes in handy. But there are also other ways to tell whether you've met someone avoidant. Arthur Conan Doyle coined the term "smoking gun" in one of his Sherlock Holmes detective novels. A smoking gun has since become a reference for an object or a fact that serves as conclusive evidence of not just a crime but any type of undeniable proof. We like to call any signal or message that is highly indicative of avoidance a smoking gun:

SMOKING GUNS THAT INDICATE YOU'RE DATING SOMEONE AVOIDANT

- **Sends mixed messages**—about his/her feelings toward you or about his/her commitment to you.
- **Longs for an ideal relationship**—*but* gives subtle hints that it will not be with you.
- **Desperately wants to meet "the one"**—*but* somehow always finds some fault in the other person or in the circumstances that makes commitment impossible.
- **Disregards your emotional well-being**—and when confronted, continues to disregard it.
- **Suggests that you are "too needy," "sensitive," or "overreacting"**—thus invalidating your feelings and making you second-guess yourself.

- **Ignores things you say that inconvenience him or her**—doesn't respond or changes the topic instead.
- **Addresses your concerns as "in a court of law"**—responding to the *facts* without taking *your feelings* into account.
- **Your messages don't get across**—despite your best efforts to communicate your needs, he or she doesn't seem to get the message or else ignores it.

Note that it is not specific behaviors that threaten to become smoking guns but rather an emotional stance—an ambiguity about the relationship that goes hand in hand with a strong message that your emotional needs are not so important to him or her. He or she may say the right things at times, but his/her actions tell a different story.

As you'll see in the next section, effective communication is an excellent tool for disarming these smoking guns.

3. A new way of dating: Be your authentic self and use effective communication.

The next step is to start *expressing* your needs. Most anxious people easily fall into the trap that relationship books—and society at large—set for them. They feel that they are too demanding and needy and so they try to accommodate their partner's need for distance and boundaries (if they're involved with someone avoidant). It's simply more socially acceptable to maintain a cool, self-sufficient façade. So they hide their wishes and mask their discontent. In actuality, you are missing out when you do so, because by expressing those needs you achieve two goals. First, you are being your authentic self, which has been found to contribute to our general feelings of happiness and fulfillment, and being happy and fulfilled is probably one of the most attractive traits you can offer a partner. Second and no less important, once you are your authentic self, if your partner is incapable of meeting your genuine needs, you can determine that early on. Not everyone has relationship needs compatible with your own, and that's fine. Let them find someone else who *wants* to be kept at arm's length, and you can go about finding someone who will make you happy.

What do we mean by "being your authentic self" and "expressing your needs"? Amir's patient Janet can illustrate this point well. At 28, she had been going out with Brian for more than a year when he decided to end the relationship. He wasn't ready to get serious and needed his space. She was absolutely devastated and couldn't stop thinking about him for many months. She wouldn't even consider dating anyone else because she still felt so connected to him. Six months later, as though in answer to her prayers, Brian called her and wanted to get back together again. Of course Janet was elated. A couple of weeks into the renewed relationship, Amir asked her how it was going. She said that they were taking things very slow and she was letting him set the pace, as she had in the past. She knew he was afraid of commitment, and she didn't want to scare him away again.

Amir strongly suggested that instead of falling into the same pattern that Brian set the first time, this time she should make her wishes absolutely clear. After all, he was the one who wanted to get back together, and he had to prove he had changed and was worthy of her love. Amir suggested spelling things out point-blank, as in "I love you very much; I need to know that you are there for me all the time. I want to know I can talk to you every day and not just when it's convenient for you. I don't want to have to cover up my wish to spend time with you for fear of driving you away."

But Janet believed that if she held out long enough, giving him his space and plenty of time, he would learn to appreciate her. That if she played it cool and self-assured, he would be more attracted to her. Perhaps not surprisingly, Janet's relationship with Brian slowly deteriorated until it finally fizzled out completely. He called less and less, continued to do as he wished without taking her well-being into account, and finally disappeared without even a real break-up talk. If Janet had let her authentic self shine through and used effective communication to voice her feelings and needs, she would have ended the sad ordeal much earlier, knowing she had given it her best shot but that Brian was simply incapable of providing what she needed. Or else Brian would have understood from day one that if he was serious about getting back together, he was going to have to rise to the occasion and take Janet's needs into account. He would know exactly what was expected of him, no guesswork required.

(For more about how to voice your authentic self using effective communication, see chapter 11.)

4. The abundance philosophy.

As we discussed earlier in the chapter, there are a disproportionate number of avoidants in the dating pool. Another useful step for successfully maneuvering through the pool is what we call the *abundance* (or "plenty of fish in the sea") *philosophy*— understanding that there are many unique and wonderful individuals out there who may be superb partners for you. Try giving several people a chance, without settling on one person very early on, making sure to give a wide berth to those with potential smoking guns.

This calls for a crucial change in your anxious thinking. You tend to assume that meeting someone suitable is an unlikely occurrence, but it doesn't have to be that way. There are many charming, intelligent people out there who can make you happy, but there are also many who are not right for you. The only way to make sure that you meet potential soul mates is to go out with a lot of people. It's a simple law of probability—the more you meet, the greater the chances you'll find the one who is a good match for you.

But it's much more than just a probability issue. If you have an anxious attachment style, you tend to get attached very quickly, even just on the basis of physical attraction. One night of sex or even just a passionate kiss and, boom, you already can't get that person out of your mind. As you know, once your attachment system is activated, you begin to crave the other person's closeness and will do anything in your power to make it work *even before you really get to know him/her and decide whether you like that person or not!* If you are seeing only him/her, the result is that at a very early stage you lose your ability to judge whether he or she is really right for you.

By using the abundance philosophy, you maintain your ability to evaluate potential partners more objectively. What you are actually doing is desensitizing your attachment system and tricking it into being easier on you. Your system will no longer get so easily activated by one person because it will be busy evaluating the availability of a lot of different people, and you won't be as likely to obsess about anyone in particular. You can quickly rule out people if they make you feel insecure or inadequate, because you haven't built all your hopes on them. Why would you waste time with someone who is unkind to you when you have several other potential partners lined up who treat you like royalty?

When you're seeing several people—which has become very feasible in the Internet and Facebook age—it also becomes easier to make your needs and wishes clear; you're not afraid that by doing so you'll chase away a rare prospect; you don't have to tiptoe around or hide your true feelings. This allows you to see whether someone is able to meet your needs *before* you reach the point of no return.

Nicky, 31, was an extreme case for whom this approach to dating worked like magic. Nicky was attractive, social, and witty, yet she rarely made it past the first few days or weeks of a relationship. She had a highly anxious attachment style; she craved intimacy and closeness but was so convinced that she would never meet anyone that being alone had become a self-fulfilling prophecy.

In romantic situations, she was very sensitive and got easily hurt and would act defensively, not returning phone calls and remaining silent (using protest behavior) until the relationship would reach a dead end. Later she would torment herself by turning things over and over in her mind (an activating strategy). It would be very difficult for her to let go and move on. Also, by keeping silent and not calling, Nicky seemed to attract a string of avoidant men who felt more comfortable with the lack of communication. But Nicky was not happy.

Finally, at our suggestion, she told all her friends to keep an eye out for potential prospects and also signed up for several online dating services. She started meeting lots of new people, thereby increasing her odds of meeting the right man—a secure man. Dating many people and not having time to get too anxious over any one particular prospect brought about a change in her attitude. Whereas before, she saw every man that she met and liked (and she was picky) as her last chance to find happiness, now prospects were plentiful. It's not that she didn't experience disappointments; some men didn't even get past the first date for one reason or another. But what did change were her anxious thought patterns—her working model for relationships:

- She saw hard evidence that many people found her attractive, even if they didn't turn out to be the perfect match. So she no longer interpreted unsuccessful dates as proof of some deep-seated problem in her. Her self-confidence increased greatly and it showed.

- When someone she was interested in started to disengage or act avoidant, she found it much easier to simply move on without losing precious time. She could say to herself, "This person is just not right for me, but the next one might be."

- When she met someone she really liked, she obsessed about him less and didn't resort as much to protest behavior. Gone (or at least reduced) were the oversensitivity and the defensiveness that made her act in self-defeating ways.

A year after her dating experiment began, she met George. He was warm and loving and he adored her. She allowed herself to open up and be vulnerable with him. These days she often jokes that in a strange twist of fate (although she knows she took an active part in making fate happen), among her friends—many of whom were in long-term relationships since college—she wound up having the happiest, most secure relationship of all!

5. Give secure people a chance.

But the abundance philosophy loses its effectiveness if you fail to recognize a keeper when you find one. Once you've recognized someone you've met as secure, remember not to make impulsive decisions about whether s/he is right for you. Remind yourself that you might feel bored at first—after all, there is less drama when your attachment system isn't activated. Give it some time. Chances are, if you are anxious, you will automatically interpret calmness in the relationship as a lack of attraction. A habit of years is not easy to shed. But if you hold out a little longer, you may start to appreciate a calm attachment system and all the advantages it has to offer.

Beware: Attachment Stereotyping

•

By dividing attachment behavior along gender lines, we can fall into the common trap of equating avoidance with masculinity. Research findings, however, prove that there are many men who are far from being avoidant—they communicate freely, are loving and affectionate, do not retreat during conflict, and are consistently there for their partner (i.e., are secure). Another misperception is that we associate the anxious attachment style with femininity when in fact most women are secure and there are plenty of men who have an anxious attachment style. However, it is important to keep in mind that there are also women who fit the avoidant description. When it comes to attachment and gender, the most important fact to remember is that the majority of the population—both male and female—are secure.

A FINAL WORD

A final word for you—the anxious reader. There is no one for whom attachment theory has more to offer than men and women with an anxious attachment style. Although you suffer the consequences of a bad match and an activated attachment system more intensely, you also stand to gain the most from understanding how the attachment system works, which relationships have the capacity to make you happy, and which situations can make you a nervous wreck. We have witnessed people who have managed to walk away from loneliness to find the companionship they longed for, using the principles outlined in this chapter. We've also witnessed people who have been in long-term relationships that brought out the worst in them, but understanding and utilizing attachment principles marked the beginning of a new phase of their relationship—a more secure phase.

6

Keeping Love at Arm's Length:
The Avoidant Attachment Style

THE LONESOME TRAVELER

Most of us are fascinated with people who go out into the world on their own, without any hindrances or obligations, without feeling the need to address or consider others' needs. From fanciful characters like Forrest Gump to real-life pioneers like Diane Fossey, such lonesome travelers often have strong principles and ideological motivations.

In Jon Krakauer's bestselling book *Into the Wild*, Chris McCandless, a superior student and athlete in his early twenties, leaves his ordinary life behind and heads for the Alaskan wilderness. Traveling alone, with minimal gear, Chris makes his way toward Alaska with the goal of living off the land without the help of other human beings. Throughout his journey, Chris engages people who want to make him a part of their lives, including an elderly man who offers to adopt him, a young girl who falls in love with him, and a couple who invites him to live with them. Chris, however, is determined to make it on his own.

Before reaching his final destination, Chris has his last human interaction with a man named Gallien who has given him a ride:

> *During the drive south toward the mountains, Gallien had tried repeatedly to dissuade Alex [Chris's pseudonym] from his plan, to no avail. He even offered to drive Alex all the way to Anchorage so he could at least buy the kid some decent gear. "No, thanks anyway," Alex replied. "I'll be fine with what I've got." When Gallien asked whether his parents or some friend knew what he was up to—anyone who could sound the alarm if he got into trouble and was overdue—Alex answered calmly that, no, nobody knew of his plans, that in fact he hadn't spoken to his family in nearly three years. "I'm absolutely positive," he assured Gallien, "I won't run into anything I can't deal with on my own."*

After parting from Gallien, Chris crosses a frozen river and ventures deep into the bush where he's completely isolated from the outside world. For several months, Chris makes it on his own, foraging and hunting for food. The next spring, however, when he tries to return home, he discovers the river is swollen with rain and melting snow, and the current is so strong that he's unable to cross back into civilization. Left with no other choice, Chris returns to his base camp, where he ultimately dies. In his last days of life, he makes the following entry in his journal: "Happiness only real when shared."

Metaphorically speaking, we view people with an avoidant attachment style as lonesome travelers on the journey of life and relationships. Like Chris, they idealize a life of self-sufficiency and look down upon dependency. If you have an avoidant attachment style, the lesson Chris ultimately learned—that experiences are only meaningful when shared with others—is key to *your* happiness as well.

In this chapter, we look at the ways in which you, the lonesome traveler, manage to keep your distance even when you're with someone you love. We help you gain insight into why you behave as you do in relationships and how that behavior is stopping you from finding true happiness in your romantic connections. If you belong to the remaining three-quarters of the population, chances are that you know—or may someday get involved with—someone avoidant. This chapter will help you understand why they act as they do.

A Survival Advantage Can't Buy You Love

•

It's believed that each attachment style evolved in order to increase the survival chances of humans in a particular environment. The secure attachment style has worked best, because throughout history our ancestors lived predominantly in close-knit groups where working together was by far the best way to secure their future and that of their offspring. To ensure the survival of the species under any condition that might arise, however, more than one strategy was called necessary. For those born into hostile conditions, in which large numbers perished from hunger, disease, or natural disasters, skills other than collaborative ones became more important. Those individuals who were able to detach and be self-sufficient were more successful at competing for limited resources in these extreme environments, and so, a segment of the population leaned toward an avoidant attachment style.

Unfortunately, the survival advantage for the human race does not necessarily translate into an advantage for the avoidant individual. Chris McCandless might still be alive if he'd been willing to collaborate with others. In fact, studies show that if you have an avoidant attachment style, you tend to be less happy and satisfied in your relationships.

The good news is that it doesn't have to be that way; you don't have to be a slave to evolutionary forces. You can learn what does not come naturally to you and improve your chances at developing a rewarding relationship.

FLYING SOLO?

It's important to remember that the avoidant attachment style always manifests itself. It determines to a great extent what you expect in relationships, how you interpret romantic situations, and how you behave with your date or partner. Whether you are single or involved in a relationship, even a committed one, you are always maneuvering to keep people at a distance.

Susan, who has an avoidant attachment style, describes herself as a free spirit. She gets involved with men—sometimes for more than a year—but then eventually tires of them, moves on to the next conquest, and jokingly refers to the "trail of broken hearts" she left behind. She sees need as a weakness and looks down on people who become dependent on their partner, mockingly referring to such situations as "jail time."

Are Susan and others with avoidant attachment styles simply devoid of the need to meaningfully connect with a significant other? And if so, doesn't that contradict the basic premise of attachment theory—that the need for physical and emotional proximity to a spouse or lover is universal?

Answering these questions isn't an easy task. Avoidants are not exactly open books and tend to repress rather than express their emotions. This is where attachment studies come in handy. Sophisticated research methods are able to reach beyond people's conscious motives and succeed where straightforward communication fails in cracking the avoidant mind-set. The following set of experiments is particularly revealing.

Six independent studies have examined how accessible attachment issues are to avoidants. They did so by measuring how long it took subjects to report words flashed quickly on a monitor. These tests operated on the well-established premise that the speed with which you report a certain word is indicative of how accessible that theme is in your mind. Researchers found that avoidants are quicker than other people to pick up on words such as "need" and "enmeshed," related to what they consider negative characteristics of their partner's behavior, but slower to recognize words like "separation," "fight," and "loss," associated with their own attachment-related worries. Avoidants, it appears, are quick to think negatively about their partners, seeing them as needy and overly dependent—a major element in their view of relationships—but ignore their own needs and fears about relationships. They seemingly despise others for being needy and are themselves immune to those needs. But is that really the case?

In the second part of these studies, researchers distracted the avoidants by giving them another task to perform—like solving a puzzle or responding to another cue—while the word recognition task was going on. In these situations, the avoidants reacted to words related to their own attachment worries ("separation," "loss," "death") just as quickly as other people did. Distracted by another task, their ability to repress lessened and their true attachment feelings and concerns were able to surface.

The experiments show that although you may be avoidant, your attachment "machinery" is still in place—making you just as vulnerable to threats of separation. Only when your mental energy is needed elsewhere and you are caught off guard, however, do these emotions and feelings emerge.

These studies also tell us that avoidants such as Susan aren't such free spirits after all; it is the defensive stance that they adopt that makes them *seem* that way. In Susan's account, notice how she makes a point of putting down those who depend on their significant others. Other studies have found that faced with a stressful life event, such as divorce, the birth of a severely disabled child, or military trauma, avoidants' defenses are quick to break down and they then appear and behave just like people with an anxious attachment style.

TOGETHER BUT APART: THE COMPROMISE THAT SATISFIES NO ONE

So how do people with an avoidant attachment style suppress their attachment needs and maintain a distance in their relationships? Let's take a closer look at the various techniques they use to keep their distance from the person closest to them—from everyday deactivating strategies to overarching perceptions and beliefs.

- Mike, 27, has spent the last five years with someone that he feels is not his intellectual equal. They love each other very much, but there's always an underlying dissatisfaction in Mike's mind about the relationship. He has a lingering feeling that something is missing and that someone better is just around the corner.
- Kaia, 31, lives with her boyfriend of two years but still reminisces about the freedom she enjoyed when she was single. She seems to have forgotten that, in actuality, she was very lonely and depressed on her own.
- Stavros, 40, a handsome and suave entrepreneur, desperately wants to get married and have kids. He knows exactly what he's looking for in a wife. She has to be young—no more than 28—good-looking, career-oriented, and no less important, she must be willing to move back with him to his hometown in Greece. After more than ten years of dating, he still hasn't found her.
- Tom, 49, married for decades to a woman he once worshipped, now feels trapped and seizes every possible op-

portunity to do things on his own—whether taking solo trips or attending events with male friends.

All of these people have one thing in common: an avoidant attachment style. They feel a deep-rooted aloneness, even while in a relationship. Whereas people with a secure attachment style find it easy to accept their partners, flaws and all, to depend on them, and to believe that they're special and unique—for avoidant people such a stance is a major life challenge. If you're avoidant, you connect with romantic partners but always maintain some mental distance and an escape route. Feeling close and complete with someone else—the emotional equivalent of finding a home—is a condition that you find difficult to accept.

DEACTIVATING STRATEGIES—YOUR EVERYDAY TOOLKIT FOR KEEPING YOUR PARTNER AT ARM'S LENGTH (OR MORE)

Although Mike, Kaia, Stavros, and Tom use different methods to disengage from their partners, they're all employing techniques known as *deactivating strategies*. A deactivating strategy is any behavior or thought that is used to squelch intimacy. These strategies suppress our attachment system, the biological mechanism in our brains responsible for our desire to seek closeness with a preferred partner. Remember the experiment in which researchers showed that avoidants have the need for closeness in a relationship but make a concerted effort to repress it? Deactivating strategies are the tools employed to suppress these needs on a day-to-day basis.

Examine the following list of deactivating strategies carefully. The more you use these tools, the more alone you'll feel and the less happy you'll be in your relationship.

Some Common Deactivating Strategies
•

- Saying (or thinking) "I'm not ready to commit"—but staying together nonetheless, sometimes for years.
- Focusing on small imperfections in your partner: the way s/he talks, dresses, eats, or (fill in the blank) and allowing it to get in the way of your romantic feelings.
- Pining after an ex-girlfriend/boyfriend—(the "phantom ex"—more on this later).
- Flirting with others—a hurtful way to introduce insecurity into the relationship.
- Not saying "I love you"—while implying that you do have feelings toward the other person.
- Pulling away when things are going well (e.g., not calling for several days after an intimate date).
- Forming relationships with an impossible future, such as with someone who is married.
- "Checking out mentally" when your partner is talking to you.
- Keeping secrets and leaving things foggy—to maintain your feeling of independence.
- Avoiding physical closeness—e.g., not wanting to share the same bed, not wanting to have sex, walking several strides ahead of your partner.

If you're avoidant, these small everyday deactivating strategies are tools you unconsciously use to make sure the person that you love (or will love) won't get in the way of your autonomy. But at the end of the day, these tools are standing in the way of *you* being happy in a relationship.

The use of deactivating strategies alone is not enough to keep attachment at bay. They're just the tip of the iceberg. As an avoidant, your mind is governed by overarching perceptions and beliefs about relationships that ensure a disconnect with your partner and get in the way of your happiness.

THOUGHT PATTERNS THAT LEAVE YOU OUT IN THE COLD

As an avoidant, you have a skewed perspective of the things that your partner says and does. The unnerving part is that you're almost entirely unconscious of these unconstructive thought patterns.

Mistaking Self-Reliance for Independence

Joe, 29: "When I was growing up, my father constantly told me not to rely on anyone. He said it so many times it became a mantra in my head: 'You can only count on yourself!' I never disputed its truth until I first went to therapy. 'Relationships? Who needs them?' I told my shrink. 'Why would I waste my time being with someone when I can only count on myself.' My therapist opened my eyes. 'That's nonsense!' he said, 'Of course you can—and should—count on other people, you do it all the time anyway. We all do.' It was one of those white-light moments. I could see that he was right. What a huge relief it was to let go of such an obsessive notion that set me apart from the rest of the world."

Joe's belief in self-reliance—and his experience of feeling alone because of it—isn't unique to him. Studies show that belief in self-reliance is very closely linked with a low degree of comfort with intimacy and closeness. Although avoidant individuals were found to have a great deal of confidence about not needing anyone else, their belief came with a price tag: They scored lowest on every measure of closeness in personal relationships. They were less willing to engage in self-disclosure, less comfortable with intimacy, and also less likely to seek help from others.

As is evident in Joe's account, a strong belief in self-reliance can be more of a burden than an asset. In romantic relationships, it reduces your ability to be close, to share intimate information, and to be in tune with your partner. Many avoidants confuse self-reliance with independence. Even though it's important for each of us to be able to stand on our own two feet, if we overrate self-reliance, we diminish the importance of getting support from other people, thus cutting ourselves off from an important lifeline.

Another problem with self-reliance is the "self" part. It forces you to ignore the needs of your partner and concentrate only on your own needs, shortchanging you of one of the most rewarding human experiences: It prevents you (and the person you love) from the joy of feeling part of something bigger than yourself.

Seeing the Worm Instead of the Apple

Another disabling thought pattern that makes you keep your partner at a distance is "seeing the worm instead of the apple." Carole had been with Bob for nine months and had been feeling increasingly unhappy. She felt Bob was the wrong guy for her, and gave a multitude of reasons: He wasn't her intellectual equal, he lacked sophistication, he was too needy, and she didn't like the way he dressed or interacted with people. Yet, at the same time, there was a tenderness about him that she'd never experienced with another man. He made her feel safe and accepted, he lavished gifts on her, and he had endless patience to deal with her silences, moods, and scorn. Still, Carole was adamant about her need to leave Bob. "It will never work," she said time and again. Finally, she broke up with him. Months later she was surprised by just how difficult she was finding things without him. Lonely, depressed, and heartbroken, she mourned their lost relationship as the best she'd ever had.

Carole's experience is typical of people with an avoidant attachment style. They tend to see the glass half-empty instead of half-full when it comes to their partner. In fact, in one study, Mario Mikulincer, dean of the New School of Psychology at the Interdisciplinary Center in Israel and one of the leading researchers in the field of adult attachment, together with colleagues Victor Florian and Gilad Hirschberger, from the department of psychology at Bar-Ilan University in Israel, asked couples to recount their daily experiences in a diary. They found that people with an avoidant attachment style rated their partner less positively than did nonavoidants. What's more, they found they did so *even on days in which their accounts of their partners' behavior indicated supportiveness, warmth, and caring.* Dr. Mikulincer explains that this pattern of behavior is driven by avoidants' generally dismissive attitude toward connectedness. When something occurs that contradicts this perspective—such as their spouse behaving in a genuinely caring and loving manner—they are prone to ignoring the behavior, or at least diminishing its value.

When they were together, Carole used many deactivating strategies, tending to focus on Bob's negative attributes. Although she was aware of her boyfriend's strengths, she couldn't keep her mind off what she perceived to be his countless flaws. Only after they broke up, and she no longer felt threatened by the high level of intimacy, did her defense strategies lift. She was then able to get in touch with the underlying feelings of attachment that were there all along and to accurately assess Bob's pluses.

CAUTION: READ THE SIGNS

Imagine if you were a parent and couldn't for the life of you read your infant's cues. You wouldn't be able to tell whether your child was hungry or tired, wanting to be held or wanting to be left alone, wet or sick. How difficult life would be for both of you. Your child would have to work so much harder—and cry so much longer—to be understood.

Having an avoidant attachment style can often make you feel like that parent. You're not strong at translating the many verbal and nonverbal signals you receive during everyday interactions into a coherent understanding of your lover's mental state. The problem is that, along with your self-reliant attitude, you also train yourself not to care about how the person closest to you is feeling. You figure that this is not your task; that they need to take care of their own emotional well-being. This lack of understanding leads partners of avoidants to complain about not receiving enough emotional support. It also leads to less connectedness, warmth, and satisfaction in the relationship.

Dr. Jeffry Simpson, professor of psychology at the University of Minnesota, studies how adult attachment orientations are associated with relationship functioning and well-being, particularly when partners are distressed. He also researches empathic accuracy—the condition under which people tend to be accurate or inaccurate in gauging their partner's feelings. In a study conducted together with Steve Rholes from Texas A & M University, they set up an experiment to examine whether people with different attachment styles differed in their abilities to infer their partners' thoughts. They asked individuals to rate the attractiveness and sexual appeal of opposite-sex images in the presence of their partners. They then asked them to assess their partners' reactions to this rating process. Avoidant individuals were found to be less accurate than anxious individuals at perceiving their partners' thoughts and feelings during the experiment. It was common for avoidants to interpret their partner's reaction as indifferent if they rated someone as highly attractive, when, in fact, their partner had been quite upset by it.

John Gray, in his enormously popular book *Men Are from Mars, Women Are from Venus*, starts out by describing the aha moment that made him write the book. Several days after his wife, Bonnie, gave birth to their baby girl in a very painful delivery, John went back to work (all signs showed she was on the mend). He came home at the end of the day, only to discover that his wife had run out of painkillers and had consequently "spent the whole day in pain, taking care of a newborn." When he saw how upset she was, he misinterpreted her distress as anger and became very defensive—trying to plead his innocence. After all, he didn't know she had run out of pills. Why hadn't she called? After a heated exchange, he was about to stomp angrily out of the house when Bonnie stopped him: "Stop, please don't leave," she said. "This is when I need you most. I'm in pain. I haven't slept in days. Please listen to me." At this point John went over to her and silently held her. Later he says: "That day, for the first time, I didn't leave her . . . I succeeded in giving to her when she really needed me."

This event—the stress and responsibility of having a newborn and his wife's highly effective communication—helped to invoke a secure working model in John. It helped bring him to the realization that his wife's well-being is his responsibility and sacred duty. This was a true revelation for him. From someone who was busy looking out for his own needs and responding defensively to his partner's requests and dissatisfactions, he managed to shift to a more secure mind-set. This is not an easy task if you have an avoidant attachment style, but it is possible if you allow yourself to open up enough to truly see your partner.

LONGING FOR THE PHANTOM EX, LOOKING FOR "THE ONE"

These are the two trickiest tools that you may be using to short-change yourself in love. You convince yourself that you have a true longing for someone from your past or that the *right* person is just around the corner and you can easily undermine yourself in love. Embracing the notion of the "perfect" partner is one of the most powerful tools an avoidant can use to keep someone else at bay. It allows you to believe that everything is fine with you and that the person you're with now is the problem—he or she is just not good enough. In addition to creating distance between you and your partner, it can also confuse him/her; when your partner hears how you miss your ex, or how you long for the perfect soul mate, it leads him/her to believe that you're craving true closeness and intimacy, when in fact you're driving it away.

The Phantom Ex

One of the consequences of devaluing your romantic relationship is that you often wake up long after the relationship has gone stale, having forgotten all those negative things that annoyed you about your partner, wondering what went wrong and reminiscing longingly about your long-lost love. We call it the *phantom-ex phenomenon*.

Often, as happened with Carole who "rediscovered" her feelings for Bob only after she'd broken up with him, once the avoidant person has put time and distance between herself and the partner whom she's lost interest in, something strange happens: The feelings of love and admiration return! Once at a safe distance, the threat of intimacy is gone and you no longer feel the need to suppress your true feelings. You can then recall all of your ex's great qualities, convincing yourself that he or she was the best partner you ever had. Of course, you can't articulate why this person wasn't right for you, or remember clearly why you ended things in the first place (or perhaps behaved so miserably that he or she had no choice but to leave). In essence, you put your past partner on a pedestal and pay tribute to "the love of your life," now forever lost. Sometimes you do try to resume the relationship, starting a vicious cycle of getting closer and withdrawing. Other times, even if the other person is available, you don't make an attempt to get back together but continue all the same to think about him or her incessantly.

This fixation with a past partner affects budding new relationships, because it acts as a deactivating strategy, blocking you from getting close to someone else. Even though you'll probably never get back together with your phantom ex, just the knowledge that they're out there is enough to make any new partner seem insignificant by comparison.

THE POWER OF "THE ONE"

Have you ever gone out with someone whom you think is amazing, but as you start to get closer, you become overwhelmed with the feeling that s/he isn't actually so hot after all? This can even happen after you've gone out with someone for a considerable amount of time or very intensively, all the while believing that s/he is the one, when all of a sudden you experience a chilling effect. You start to notice she has a weird way of eating, or that his nose blowing infuriates you. You end up discovering that after the initial exhilaration, you feel suffocated and need to take a step back. What you don't realize is that this surge of negativity could in fact be a deactivating strategy, unconsciously triggered to turn off your attachment needs.

Not wanting to look inward—and believing that we all have the same capacity for intimacy—you conclude that you're just not in love enough and so pull away. You partner is crushed and protests, but this only strengthens your conviction that s/he is not "the one." Moving from one date to the next, you begin this vicious cycle over and over, believing all along that once you find "the one," you'll effortlessly connect on a totally different level.

CAN AVOIDANTS CHANGE?

As you read this chapter, it becomes apparent that being avoidant isn't really about living a self-sufficient life; it's about a life of struggle involving the constant suppression of a powerful attachment system using the (also powerful) deactivating strategies we've outlined. Because of their power it's easy to conclude that these behaviors, thoughts, and beliefs are impossible to uproot and change. But, strictly speaking, this is not the case. What *is* true is that people with an avoidant attachment style overwhelmingly assume that the reason they're unable to find happiness in a relationship has little to do with themselves and a lot to do with external circumstances—meeting the wrong people, not finding "the one," or only hooking up with prospects who want to tie them down. They rarely search inside themselves for the reason for their dissatisfaction, and even more rarely seek help or even agree to get help when their partner suggests they do so. Unfortunately, until they look inward or seek counseling, change is not likely to occur.

On occasions when avoidants reach a low point in their life—because of severe loneliness, a life-altering experience, or a major accident—they can change their way of thinking. For those of you who have reached that point, take note of the following eight actions that will get you one step closer to true intimacy. Most of these steps require, first and foremost, increasing your self-awareness. But knowing about the thought patterns that deny you the ability to truly get close to someone is only the first step. The next and *harder* step requires you to start to identify instances in which you employ these attitudes and behaviors, and then to embark on the voyage of change.

COACHING SESSION: EIGHT THINGS YOU CAN START DOING TODAY TO STOP PUSHING LOVE AWAY

1. **Learn to identify deactivating strategies.** Don't act on your impulse. When you're excited about someone but then suddenly have a gut feeling that s/he is not right for you, stop and think. Is this actually a deactivating strategy? Are all those small imperfections you're starting to notice really your attachment system's way of making you step back? Remind yourself that this picture is skewed and that you need intimacy despite your discom-

fort with it. If you thought s/he was great to begin with, you have a lot to lose by pushing him or her away.

2. **De-emphasize self-reliance and focus on mutual support.** When your partner feels s/he has a secure base to fall back on (and doesn't feel the need to work hard to get close), and when you don't feel the need to distance yourself, you'll both be better able to look outward and do your own thing. You'll become more independent and your partner will be less needy. (See more on the "dependency paradox" in chapter 2).

3. **Find a secure partner.** As you will see in chapter 7, people with secure attachment styles tend to make their anxious and avoidant partners more secure as well. Someone with an anxious attachment style, however, will exacerbate your avoidance—often in a perpetual vicious cycle. Given a chance, we recommend you choose the secure route. You'll experience less defensiveness, less fighting, and less anguish.

4. **Be aware of your tendency to misinterpret behaviors.** Negative views of your partner's behaviors and intentions infuse bad vibes into the relationship. Change this pattern! Recognize this tendency, notice when it happens, and look for a more plausible perspective. Remind yourself that this is your partner, you chose to be together, and that maybe you're better off trusting that they do have your best interests at heart.

5. **Make a relationship gratitude list.** Remind yourself on a daily basis that you tend to think negatively of your partner or date. It is simply part of your makeup if you

have an avoidant attachment style. Your objective should be to notice the positive in your partner's actions. This may not be an easy task, but with practice and perseverance, you'll gradually get the hang of it. Take time every evening to think back on the events of the day. List at least one way your partner contributed, even in a minor way, to your well-being, and why you're grateful they're in your life.

6. **Nix the phantom ex.** When you find yourself idealizing that one special ex-partner, stop and acknowledge that he or she is not (and never was) a viable option. By remembering how critical you were of that relationship—and how leery you were of committing—you can stop using him or her as a deactivating strategy and focus on someone new.

7. **Forget about "the one."** We don't dispute the presence of soul mates in our world. On the contrary, we wholeheartedly believe in the soul mate experience. But it is our belief that you have to be an active party in the process. Don't wait until "the one" who fits your checklist shows up and then expect everything to fall into place. *Make* them into your soul mate by choosing them out of the crowd, allowing them to get close (using the strategies we offer in this chapter) and making them a special part of you.

8. **Adopt the distraction strategy.** As an avoidant, it's easier to get close to your partner if there's a distraction (remember the experiment with a distraction task). Focusing on other things—taking a hike, going sailing, or prepar-

ing a meal together—will allow you to let your guard down and make it easier to access your loving feelings. Use this little trick to promote closeness in your time together.

For additional avoidance-busting tips, see chapter 8.

7.

Getting Comfortably Close: The Secure Attachment Style

Writing about people with a secure attachment style seems like a boring task. After all, what is there to say? If you're secure, you're very reliable, consistent, and trustworthy. You don't try to dodge intimacy or go nuts over your relationships. There's very little drama in your romantic ties—no high and lows, no yo-yos and roller coasters to speak of. So what is there to say?"

Actually, there's a lot to say! In the process of understanding attachment and how a secure bond can transform someone's life, we've grown to admire and appreciate the secures of the world. They're attuned to their partners' emotional and physical cues and know how to respond to them. Their emotional system doesn't get too riled up in the face of threat (as with the anxious) but doesn't get shut down either (as with the avoidant). In this chapter, you'll learn more about the secure traits and what makes them unique. And if you're secure and don't usually seek help in the relationship arena, you'll be forewarned because you too may one day stumble into an ineffective relationship that can affect you in a deleterious way.

THE SECURE BUFFERING EFFECT

Time and again, research shows that the best predictor of happiness in a relationship is a secure attachment style. Studies demonstrate that individuals with a secure attachment style report higher levels of satisfaction in their relationships than people with other attachment styles. Patrick Keelan, as part of his doctoral dissertation at the University of Toronto, conducted a study to test this issue. Together with the late psychology professor Kenneth Dion and his longtime research partner and wife, Karen Dion, a psychology professor at the University of Toronto, they followed over one hundred university students who were in dating relationships over a four-month period. They found that secure individuals maintained high levels of relationship satisfaction, commitment, and trust. In contrast, insecure individuals reported decreasing levels of all three over the same four months.

But what happens when secure and insecure interact? In a separate experiment, researchers got observers to rate couples' functioning during a joint interaction. It's no surprise that secure couples—those in which both partners were secure—functioned better than insecure couples—those in which both partners were either anxious or avoidant. But what was more interesting was that there was no observed difference between secure couples and "mixed" couples—

those with only one secure partner. They both showed less conflict and were rated as better functioning than were the "insecure" dyads.

So not only do people with a secure attachment style fare better in relationships, they also create a buffering effect, somehow managing to raise their insecure partner's relationship satisfaction and functioning to their own high level. This is a very important finding. It means that if you're with someone secure, they nurture you into a more secure stance.

TELL ME, IS IT MAGIC?

What is it about people with a secure attachment style that creates this "magical" effect on their relationships? Are secures always the most friendly, likable, or sociable people around? Can you recognize them on the basis of their charm, composure, or self-confidence? The answer to all these questions is no. As with the other attachment styles, personality or physical traits won't give secures away. Secure people fit almost every description across the personality spectrum:

- Aaron, 30, a chemical engineer, is an introvert with a strong dislike of social events. He spends most of his free time working, reading, or with his brothers and parents and finds it hard to make new connections. He had his first sexual experience two years ago.
- Brenda, 27, a movie producer, acts as a social hub, knows everyone, and is always where the action is. She had one

serious boyfriend from age 18 to 24 and has been seeing other people ever since.

- Gregory, 50, an electrical engineer and divorced father of two, is very outgoing and easy to get along with. He's still licking his wounds from his failed marriage and is on the lookout for wife number two.

Secures come in every possible shape, size, and form. Something else distinguishes them that is harder to recognize, at least at first. Janet, 41, experienced that "something" firsthand:

Overwhelmed by the amount of work she'd left unfinished before the weekend, Janet woke up Monday morning in a state of dread. She was convinced that there was no way she'd ever get through the enormous pile on her desk, and her situation made her feel incompetent. She turned to her husband, Stan, who was lying in bed besides her and—out of nowhere—told him how disappointed she was with *his* business's progress and how worried she was that *he* wasn't going to make it. Stan was taken aback, but responded to Janet's attack without any visible trace of animosity. "I understand that you're frightened and there might be some comfort for you if I feel frightened too, but if you're trying to encourage me to be more efficient at work—which you often do—this isn't the best way to do it."

Janet was dumbfounded. She knew he was right—that she'd been expressing only her own concerns. Seeing that she was tearful, Stan offered to drive her to work. In the car, she apologized. She hadn't meant the stuff she'd said, but she was in such an emotional funk that everything seemed dreary to her.

It was then that she realized what a wonderfully supportive husband Stan was. If *he* had attacked *her* out of the blue, she'd have struck back and World War III would have broken out. She wouldn't have stayed collected enough to see what was really going on, to understand that it wasn't about her but about him. Stan's ability to handle the situation in the way he did required a real emotional gift. "I have to remember how good it feels to be on the receiving end of that and offer some in return someday," she thought to herself.

WHEN THREAT GOES UNDETECTED

People with a secure attachment style, like Stan, are characterized by something very real but not outwardly visible—they are programmed to expect their partners to be loving and responsive and don't worry much about losing their partners' love. They feel extremely comfortable with intimacy and closeness and have an uncanny ability to communicate their needs and respond to their partners' needs.

In fact, a series of studies aimed at accessing subjects' unconscious minds (by measuring how long it takes them to report words that flash quickly on a monitor, as described in chapter 6) compared the reactions of people with anxious, avoidant, and secure attachment styles. The studies found that secures have more unconscious access to themes such as love, hugs, and closeness and less access to danger, loss, and separation. The negative threatening themes didn't get through to them as easily. However, unlike avoidants, who didn't react to these words initially but did react to them when they were distracted by another task, secures continued to overlook them even in the distraction condition. Unlike people with an avoidant attachment style, secures aren't concerned with threatening relationship thoughts even when they are caught off guard. In other words, they don't have to make an effort to repress these ideas; they simply aren't worried about these issues—either consciously or subconsciously! What's more, when secures were specifically—and in this experiment, consciously—asked to think about separation, abandonment, and loss, they succeeded in doing so and did become more nervous as a result, as measured by skin conductance tests (which measure the amount of sweat on the skin). Remarkably, though, when they were told to stop thinking about these topics, their skin conductance abruptly went back to normal. So it seems that what may come as hard work for some—to keep an even emotional keel in the face of threat—comes effortlessly for someone secure. They simply aren't as sensitive to the negative cues of the world.

This stance influences every aspect of their romantic relationships. They are:

- **Great conflict busters**—During a fight they don't feel the need to act defensively or to injure or punish their partner, and so prevent the situation from escalating.
- **Mentally flexible**—They are not threatened by criticism. They're willing to reconsider their ways, and if necessary, revise their beliefs and strategies.
- **Effective communicators**—They expect others to be understanding and responsive, so expressing their feelings freely and accurately to their partners comes naturally to them.
- **Not game players**—They want closeness and believe others want the same, so why play games?

- **Comfortable with closeness, unconcerned about boundaries**—They seek intimacy and aren't afraid of being "enmeshed." Because they aren't overwhelmed by a fear of being slighted (as are the anxious) or the need to deactivate (as are the avoidants), they find it easy to enjoy closeness, whether physical or emotional.

- **Quick to forgive**—They assume their partners' intentions are good and are therefore likely to forgive them when they do something hurtful.

- **Inclined to view sex and emotional intimacy as one**— They don't need to create distance by separating the two (by being close either emotionally *or* sexually but not both).

- **Treat their partners like royalty**—When you've become part of their inner circle, they treat you with love and respect.

- **Secure in their power to improve the relationship**— They are confident in their positive beliefs about themselves and others, which makes this assumption logical.

- **Responsible for their partners' well-being**—They expect others to be responsive and loving toward them and so are responsive to others' needs.

Many people who live with insecure partners cannot even begin to imagine how fundamentally different life with a secure person can be. For starters, they don't engage in the "relationship dance" that therapists often refer to—whereby one partner gets closer while the other steps back in order to maintain a certain distance in the relationship at all times. Instead there's a feeling of growing closeness and intimacy. Second, they are able to sensitively and empathically—and most important, coherently—discuss their emotions with you. Last, the secure party engulfs his or her partner in an emotionally protective shield that makes facing the outside world an easier task. We often fail to realize what a bonus these attributes are unless they're missing. It's no coincidence that the people most appreciative of a secure relationship are those who've had relationships with both secure *and* insecure partners. Though these people will tell you that secure and insecure relationships are worlds apart, without the knowledge of attachment theory, they too are unable to put their finger on what exactly that difference is.

WHERE DOES THIS "TALENT" COME FROM?

If you are secure, are you born with this exceptional capacity or is it something you learn along the way? John Bowlby believed that attachment styles are a function of life experience—especially of our interaction with our parents during infancy. A person will develop a secure attachment style if her parents are sensitive and responsive to her needs. Such a child will learn that she can rely on her parents, confident that they'll be available to her whenever she needs them. But Bowlby maintained that it didn't end there; he believed a secure child would carry this confidence into adulthood and future relationships with romantic partners.

Does the evidence support these predictions? In 2000, Leslie Atkinson, who conducts child development research at Ryerson University in Toronto, in collaboration with several other colleagues, conducted a meta-analysis that was based on forty-one prior studies. In total, the study analyzed over two thousand parent-child pairs to evaluate the connection between parent sensitivity and child attachment style. The results showed a weak but significant link between the two—children of mothers who were sensitive to their needs *were* more likely to have a secure attachment style, but the weak link means that, aside from methodological issues, there could be many other variables that come into play to determine a child's attachment style. Among the factors that were found to increase a child's chance of being secure were an easy temperament (which makes it easier for parents to be responsive), positive maternal conditions—marital satisfaction, low stress and depression, and social support—and fewer hours with a nonparental caretaker.

To complicate matters further, an idea that has been gaining scientific momentum in recent years is that we are genetically predisposed toward a certain attachment style. In a genetic association study, which examines whether a particular variant of a gene is more prevalent with one specific trait than with another, Omri Gillath, from the University of Kansas, and his colleagues from the University of California, Davis, discovered that a specific pattern of the dopamine receptor DRD2 allele is associated with the anxious attachment style, whereas a variant of the serotonin 5-HT1A receptor was linked to avoidance. These two genes are known to play a role in many brain functions, including emotions, reward, attention, and importantly, also in social behavior and pair bonding. The authors conclude that "attachment insecurities are partially explained by particular genes, although there is still a great deal of individual difference variance that remains to be explained by other genes or social experiences." In other words, genes may play an important role in determining our attachment style.

But even if we were secure in infancy, will it last into adulthood? To test this question, attachment researchers reassessed subjects who had been infants in the 1970s and 1980s and were now around 20 years old. Would the men and women classified as secure in early childhood remain secure as adults? The answer remains unclear: Three studies failed to find a correlation between attachment security in infancy and in adulthood, while two other studies did find a statistically significant connection between the two. What is clear is that even if there is a correlation between attachment style in childhood and in adulthood, it is weak at best.

So where *does* the secure attachment come from? As more studies become available, there is increasing evidence that a secure attachment style doesn't originate from a single source. The equation of a caring and sensitive parent producing a secure-for-life child is too one-dimensional; instead it seems that an entire mosaic of factors comes together to create this attachment pattern: our early connection with our parents, our genes, and also something else—our romantic experiences as adults. On average, about 70 to 75 percent of adults remain consistently in the same attachment category at different points in their lives, while the remaining 30 to 25 to 30 percent of the population report a change in their attachment style.

Researchers attribute this change to romantic relationships in adulthood that are so powerful that they actually revise our most basic beliefs and attitudes toward connectedness. And yes, that change can happen in both directions—secure people can become less secure and people who were originally insecure can become increasingly secure. If you are insecure, this piece of information is vital and could be your ticket to happiness in relationships. If you are secure, you should be aware of this finding because you have a lot to lose by becoming less secure.

Tapping Into the Secure Mind-set—
Creating a Secure Base for Your Partner

•

As you recall, one of the most important roles we play in our partners' lives is providing a secure base: creating the conditions that enable our partners to pursue their interests and explore the world in confidence. Brooke Feeney and Roxanne Thrush, of Carnegie Mellon University, in a study published in 2010, found that three specific behaviors underlie this broad term. You too can provide a secure base by adopting the following secure behaviors:

- **Be available:** Respond sensitively to their distress, allow them to be dependent on you when they feel the need, check in with them from time to time, and provide comfort when things go wrong.
- **Don't interfere:** Provide *behind-the-scenes* support for their endeavors. Help in a way that leaves them with the initiative and the feeling of power. Allow them to do their own thing without trying to take over the situation, micromanage, or undermine their confidence and abilities.
- **Encourage:** Provide encouragement and be accepting of their learning and personal growth goals. Boost their self-esteem.

IT'S NOT ME; IT'S YOU— CHOOSING A PARTNER

If you have a secure attachment style, you know how to sidestep many of the obstacles that people with other attachment styles have difficulty dealing with. You naturally gravitate toward those with the capacity to make you happy. Unlike the anxious, you don't let an activated attachment system distract you—you aren't addicted to the highs and lows of being with someone who keeps you guessing all the time. Unlike avoidants, you aren't diverted by false fantasies of the perfect person waiting for you or "the one" that got away, and you don't unconsciously employ deactivating strategies that cause you to get cold feet when someone starts to get close.

As a secure, the opposite is true of you—you believe that there are many potential partners open to intimacy and closeness who would be responsive to your needs. You know you deserve to be loved and valued at all times. You are *programmed* to expect that. If someone sends out vibes that are *not* in line with these expectations—if they're inconsistent or evasive—you automatically lose interest. Tanya, 28, a secure woman we interviewed, put it very simply:

"I've slept with eleven guys in my life and they've all wanted to have a serious relationship with me. I guess it's something I convey. I know that I get the message across that I'm someone who's worth getting to know, not just in bed, that if they stick around, there's a treasure to be revealed.

"The guys I show interest in don't play games—that is very important to me. They call immediately the next day, or at the very latest

the next evening. In return, right from the start I show them that I'm interested. There were only two men in my life that waited two days to call, and I screened them both out immediately."

Notice that Tanya wastes no time at all on men she perceives as not being responsive enough to her needs. To some, her decisions might seem rash, but for secure people such behavior comes naturally. Studies in the field of attachment have confirmed that subjects with a more secure attachment style are indeed less likely to play games. Tanya knows intuitively which partners are wrong for her. Game playing is a deal breaker as far as she is concerned. The important thing about her approach is that Tanya assumes that if her partner treats her disrespectfully, it's indicative of *his* inability to be responsive in a relationship, and *not* of her own worth. She also doesn't have too many negative feelings about these two men. It's just a nonissue for her, and she instinctively moves on. This is very different from someone anxious who would probably assume that she was to blame for her date's actions. She might start to second-guess her own behavior—"I must have come on too strong," "I should have invited him up," or "It was so stupid to ask about his ex"—giving the wrong people a second, third, or fourth chance.

In Tanya's case, she'd seen enough and found it pointless to move forward with men she could tell were unable to meet her emotional needs. But in case of doubt, one of the tools most frequently used by people with a secure attachment style is *effective communication*—they simply surface their feelings and see how their date reacts. If their partner shows true concern for their well-being and a willingness to find a middle ground, they'll give the relationship a chance. If not, they won't stick around to fight what they believe to be a losing battle (see chapter 11).

Finding the Right Partner—the *Secure* Way

·

The principles we advocate throughout this book for finding the right partner are employed intuitively by people with a secure attachment style. They include:

- Spotting "smoking guns" very early on and treating them as deal breakers.
- Effectively communicating your needs from day one.
- Subscribing to the belief that there are many (yes, many!) potential partners who could make you happy.
- Never taking blame for a date's offensive behavior. When a partner acts inconsiderately or hurtfully, secures acknowledge that it says a lot about the other person rather than about themselves.
- Expecting to be treated with respect, dignity, and love.

DOES THIS MEAN THAT SECURES ARE IMMUNE TO RELATIONSHIP PROBLEMS?

Secure people don't always hook up with one another—they date and marry people of all three attachment styles. The good news is that if you're secure, you have the potential to get along with people who have anxious or avoidant attachment styles—but only if you are able to maintain your secure frame of mind. If you find yourself becoming less secure, not only do you lose a priceless gift, but you also experience less happiness and satisfaction in your relationships.

If you're secure, one of the reasons you're able to maintain a satisfying relationship with someone who has an insecure attachment style is because he or she will gradually become more secure as a result of being with you. When you date someone anxious, this is most often what happens. One of the things that Mary Ainsworth observed in the mother-infant relationship was that secure mothers were a special breed. It's not that they tended more to their children, or held them more than mothers of anxious or avoidant children, but they seemed to possess a kind of "sixth sense" and intuitively knew *when* the child wanted to be held. They sensed their child's emerging distress and acted on it before it turned into a full-blown fit. And if the child did get distressed, they just seemed to know how to soothe her.

We find this phenomenon in adult couples too. Secure adults naturally know how to soothe their partners and take care of them—it's an innate talent. This can be seen in the couple's transition to parenthood. Jeffry Simpson from the University of Minnesota and Steven Rholes from Texas A&M University—coeditors of the book *Attachment Theory and Close Relationships*, together with Lorne Campbell and Carol Wilson—found that during the shift into parenthood, anxiously attached women were more likely to move toward security in their interactions with their partners if they perceived their spouses as available, supportive, and accepting during pregnancy—all secure traits. In other words, secure adults' sensitivity and encouragement have the same effect on their partners as the secure mother's on her infant, enough to create a shift in their partners' attachment style.

A word of caution, however. Sometimes secure people, despite their innate talent for warding off potentially unsuitable matches and making their partners more secure, can find themselves in bad relationships. This can happen not only when they're inexperienced but also when they respond to their long-term partner's unacceptable behavior, by continuing to give them the benefit of the doubt and tolerate their actions.

Nathan, 35, was at his wits' end. In the eight years since he'd married Shelly, things had gone from bad to worse. Shelly's temper tantrums, rare at first, now occurred almost daily. Her outbursts also increased in severity; she broke household objects and on one occasion even slapped him. But the problems in their relationship didn't end there. Nathan not only caught her having online affairs, but strongly suspected that she was having real-life ones as well. Though Shelly threatened to leave many times—almost as if she was testing Nathan's patience and tolerance—she didn't pick up and move out. He was sure that once this "period" was over, everything would return to normal. He also saw himself as responsible for Shelly's well-being and didn't want to abandon her when she was going through such a "rough patch." So he put up with the abuse and the affairs. Finally, Shelly announced that she no longer loved him, had met someone else, and was ending the marriage. Once Shelly decided to leave, Nathan accepted her decision and didn't try to win her back.

Now with the divorce behind him, Nathan is relieved that Shelly took matters into her own hands and freed him from a difficult existence. He's even open to meeting a new person and making her part of his life. But he still finds it hard to explain what kept him there for so long. Attachment theory offers an explanation. For one, as we've seen, people with a secure attachment style view their partners' well-being as their responsibility. As long as they have reason to believe their partner is in some sort of trouble, they'll continue to back him or her. Mario Mikulincer and Phillip Shaver, in their book *Attachment in Adulthood*, show that people with a secure attachment style are more likely than others to forgive their partner for wrongdoing. They explain this as a complex combination of cognitive and emotional abilities: "Forgiveness requires difficult regulatory maneuvers . . . understanding a transgressor's needs and motives, and making generous attributions and appraisals concerning the transgressor's traits and hurtful actions. . . . Secure people are likely to offer relatively benign explanations of their partners' hurtful actions and be inclined to forgive the partner." Also, as we've seen previously in this chapter, secure people just naturally dwell less on the negative and can turn off upsetting emotions without becoming defensively distant.

The good news is that people with a secure attachment style have healthy instincts and usually catch on very early that someone is not cut out to be their partner. The bad news is that when secure people do, on occasion, enter into a negative relationship, they might not know when to call it quits—especially if it's a long-term, committed relationship in which they feel responsible for their partner's happiness.

HOW CAN YOU TELL IF THINGS HAVE GONE TOO FAR?

If you're secure but start to feel agitated, worried, or jealous (anxious traits), or if you find yourself thinking twice before expressing your feelings, or are becoming less trusting of or starting to play games with your partner (avoidant traits), it is a huge warning sign and very likely that you're with the wrong person or that you've been through a difficult experience that has shaken the core of your secure foundation. Life events such as the loss of a loved one, an illness, or a divorce can cause such a shift.

If you're still in the relationship, remember that just because you *can* get along with anyone doesn't mean you *have* to. If you're unhappy after having tried every way to make things work, chances are that you should move on. It's in your best interest to end a dysfunctional relationship rather than get stuck forever with the wrong person just because you're secure.

If you've experienced loss of an attachment figure, for whatever reason, remember that it wasn't your set of beliefs that were to blame and it is well worth holding on to them. It is better to find a way to heal the wounds and maintain the hope that there are other people out there who share your need for intimacy and closeness. You *can* be happy again.

A FINAL WORD OF RECOGNITION FOR THE SECURES OF THIS WORLD

Before we learned about attachment theory, we took the secures of the world for granted, and even dismissed them as boring. But looking through the attachment prism, we've come to appreciate secure people's talents and abilities. The goofy Homer Simpson–like colleague whom we barely noticed was suddenly transformed into a guy with impressive relationship talent who treats his wife admirably, and our get-a-life neighbor suddenly became a perceptive, caring person who keeps the entire family emotionally in check. But not all secure people are homebodies or goofy. You are not settling by going secure! Secures come in all shapes and forms. Many are good-looking and sexy. Whether plain or gorgeous, we've learned to appreciate them all for what they really are—the "super-mates" of evolution—and we hope that you will too.

PART THREE

When Attachment
Styles Clash

8.

The Anxious–Avoidant Trap

Wwhen the two people in a couple have colliding intimacy needs, their relationship is likely to become more of a storm-tossed voyage than a safe haven. Here are three examples of what we mean.

THE DIRTY LAUNDRY

Janet, 37, and Mark, 40, have been living together for almost eight years. For the past two years they've been having an ongoing dispute about whether to buy a washing machine. Mark is strongly in favor— it will save them a lot of time and hassle. Janet is adamantly opposed—their Manhattan apartment is tiny, and fitting in another appliance will mean cramping their style even more. Besides, as she sees it, she's responsible for the laundry, so why is Mark making such a big deal about it? When they discuss the subject, they both become highly emotional and it usually ends by Janet clamming up or Mark exploding.

What are they fighting about?

To get at the real issue, let's add the following piece of information to the equation: When Janet does the laundry, it's on weekends and she goes to her sister's place around the block. This is the sensible thing to do—her sister has a washing machine, it's free and less trouble. She then idles away the entire day there. Janet has an avoidant attachment style and is always finding opportunities to do things without Mark. For Mark, who has an anxious attachment style, the desire for a washing machine is really a wish for something else altogether—to be close to Janet.

When viewed in this light, we can see that the washing machine dispute is only a symptom of the *real* issue—the fact that Mark and Janet have very different needs when it comes to closeness and spending time together.

A ROMANTIC BED-AND-BREAKFAST IN VERMONT

Susan, 24, and Paul, 28, decide to go on a spontaneous weekend trip to Vermont. When they get there, they check out two B&Bs. Both places are cozy and inviting. One has a room with two single beds and the other has a room with one large queen-size bed. Paul wants the room with the two single beds, because the view is spectacular. Susan wants the one with the large bed—she can't imagine going on a romantic getaway and having to sleep in a separate bed. Paul is a little dismissive of Susan. "We sleep in the same bed every night, what's the big deal? At least we can enjoy the view here." Susan feels ashamed that she has this strong need to be close to Paul at night, but still, she just can't imagine them sleeping in separate beds on their vacation. Neither wants to give in, and the argument threatens to spoil the weekend.

What is this disagreement about? On the face of it, a difference in taste when it comes to hotel rooms. Susan's insistence seems a bit extreme. But what if you knew that Paul hates to cuddle with her before going to sleep? That this bothers Susan greatly and that she feels rejected by his behavior? What if you knew that she's sure that with two separate beds he will rush to his own the minute the sex is over? In this fuller context, she doesn't seem so unreasonable anymore. We can interpret her concern as a fundamental need for closeness that is going unmet.

WHEN FACEBOOK AND "ABANDONMENT" ISSUES MEET

Naomi, 33, and Kevin, 30, have been seeing each other exclusively for six months and have a couple of disagreements they can't resolve. Naomi is upset that Kevin hasn't "unfriended" a couple of ex-girlfriends from his list on Facebook. She is convinced he is flirting with other women. Kevin, on the other hand, doesn't like the fact that Naomi makes a habit of calling him whenever he's out having drinks with his pals, so he screens her calls. Kevin believes that Naomi has serious abandonment issues and is overly jealous—and he frequently tells her so. Naomi tries to control her gnawing doubts and worries, but they just won't go away.

There is no hard and fast relationship rule about keeping ex-girlfriends on your Facebook account or remaining in touch with them. There is also no right or wrong when it comes to phoning your boyfriend when he's out with friends. In certain situations, these behaviors might make perfect sense. But Naomi and Kevin's disagreements are not really about these questions at all, and that is why they're unable to reach a resolution. Their conflict is about how close and committed they want to be to each other. Kevin, who has an avoidant attachment style, wants to keep a certain distance between himself and Naomi, and he does so using various strategies—he remains secretive about his comings and goings and he stays in touch with old flames despite Naomi's obvious discomfort. Naomi, for her part, tries to get closer to Kevin by eliminating the barriers and distractions he has placed between them. But without his genuine desire to get closer, her efforts are futile; after all, it takes two willing individuals to create intimacy.

All three cases we've described have one thing in common: While one partner truly wants intimacy, the other feels very uncomfortable when things become too close. This is often the case when one of the partners in a bond is avoidant and the other is either anxious or secure—but it's most pronounced when one partner is avoidant and the other anxious.

Research on attachment repeatedly shows that when your need for intimacy is met and reciprocated by your partner, your satisfaction level will rise. Incongruent intimacy needs, on the other hand, usually translate into substantially lower satisfaction. When couples disagree about the degree of closeness and intimacy desired in a relationship, the issue eventually threatens to dominate all of their dialogue. We call this situation the "anxious-avoidant trap," because like a trap, you fall into it with no awareness, and like a trap, once you're caught, it's hard to break free.

The reason people in an anxious-avoidant relationship find it particularly hard to move toward more security is primarily because they are trapped in a cycle of exacerbating each other's insecurities. Take a look at the diagram on page 158. People with an anxious attachment style (lower circle on the right) cope with threats to the relationship by activating their attachment system—trying to get close to their partner. People who are avoidant (lower circle on the left) have the opposite reaction. They cope with threats by deactivating—taking measures to distance themselves from their partners and "turn off" their attachment system. Thus the closer the anxious tries to get, the more distant the avoidant acts. To make matters worse, one partner's activation further reinforces the other's deactivation in a vicious cycle, and they both remain within the relationship "danger zone." In order to move toward more security—the safe zone in the diagram—both members of the couple need to find a way to feel less threatened, get less activated/deactivated, and get out of the danger zone.

THE NUTS AND BOLTS OF THE ANXIOUS-AVOIDANT TRAP

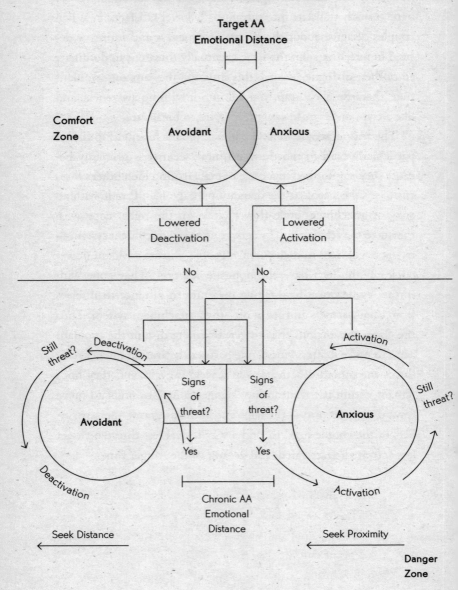

Here is what characteristically happens in many anxious-avoidant relationships:

TELLTALE SIGNS OF THE ANXIOUS-AVOIDANT TRAP

1. **The roller-coaster effect.** In the relationship you never sail along on an even keel. Instead, every once in a while, when the avoidant partner makes him/herself available to the anxious partner, the latter's attachment system is temporarily quieted and you achieve extreme closeness—leading to the feeling of a "high." This closeness, however, is perceived as a threat by the avoidant partner and is quickly followed by withdrawal on his or her part—only to create renewed dissatisfaction for the anxious partner.

2. **The emotional counterbalancing act.** If you're avoidant, you often inflate your self-esteem and sense of independence in comparison to someone else. If you're anxious, you are programmed to feel "less than" when your attachment system gets activated. Frequently avoidants feel independent and powerful only to the extent that their partner feels needy and incapable. This is one of the main reasons avoidants hardly ever date one another. They can't feel strong and independent in relation to someone who shares the same sentiment as they do.

3. **Stable instability.** The relationship may last for a long time, but an element of uncertainty persists. As illustrated on page 158, you may remain together but with a feeling of chronic dissatisfaction, never finding the degree of intimacy that you are both comfortable with.

4. **Are we really fighting about this?** You may feel that you're constantly fighting about things you shouldn't be fighting about at all. In fact, your fights aren't about these minor problems but about something else altogether—the amount of intimacy between you.

5. **Life in the inner circle as the enemy.** If you are anxious, you find that you're getting treated worse instead of better once you become the person closest to the avoidant partner. We'll explore this further in the next chapter.

6. **Experiencing the trap.** You develop the eerie sense that the relationship is not right for you, but you feel too emotionally connected to the other person to leave.

WHY ARE INTIMACY DIFFERENCES SO DIFFICULT TO RECONCILE?

If two people are in love, can't they find a way to be together and work out their differences? We wish the answer was a simple yes, but we've often seen that it's impossible to find a resolution acceptable to both the anxious partner and the avoidant partner, regardless of how much love they feel for each other. Typically, if the relationship runs its usual course (we will show you later that this does not have to be so) despite differing intimacy needs, the anxious partner is usually the one who has to make concessions and accept the rules imposed by the avoidant partner.

So even if the relationship is left to its own devices and lasts for a long time (in a stably unstable manner), without an attempt to steer it toward a secure place, things don't usually get better—and may get worse. Here's why:

- Intimacy differences can spill over into more and more areas of life—radically different intimacy needs don't stop with seemingly trivial matters like one person wanting to hold hands more often than the other. These differences reflect diametrically opposed desires, assumptions, and attitudes. In fact, they affect almost every aspect of a shared life; from the way you sleep together to how you raise your children. With every new development in the relationship (getting married, having kids, moving to a new home, making money, or becoming ill) these basic differences will manifest themselves, and the gap between partners may widen as the challenges become greater.

- Conflict is often left unresolved because the resolution itself creates too much intimacy. If you are anxious or secure, you genuinely want to work out a relationship problem. However, the resolution itself often brings a couple closer together—this is a scenario that, however unconsciously, the avoidant partner wants to avoid. While people with an anxious or secure attachment style seek to resolve a disagreement to achieve greater emotional closeness, this outcome is uncomfortable for the avoidant who actually seeks to remain distant. In order to dodge the possibility of getting closer, avoidants tend to grow more hostile and distant as arguments progress. Unless there is recognition of the process involved in an anxious-avoidant conflict, the distancing during conflict tends to repeat itself and causes a lot of unhappiness. Without addressing the issue, the situation can go from bad to worse.

- With every clash, the anxious person loses more ground: During bitter fights between anxious and avoidant partners, when there are no secure checks and balances in place, people with anxious attachment style tend to get overwhelmed by negative emotions. When they feel hurt, they talk, think, and act in an extreme manner, even to the point of threatening to leave (protest behavior). However, once they calm down, they become flooded with positive memories and are then overcome with regret. They reach out to their partner in an attempt to reconcile. But they are often met with a hostile response, because avoidants react differently to a fight. They turn off all attachment-related memories and remember the worst of their partner.

What often happens at this point, if you are anxious, is that you not only fail to resolve the *original* conflict but now find yourself in a worse position than you were in the first place. Now you have to plead just to return to your initial, unsatisfactory status quo (and often have to compromise for less). Any hopes for a better life together get washed down the drain.

9

Escaping the Anxious-Avoidant Trap: How the Anxious-Avoidant Couple Can Find Greater Security

f you've discovered that most of your difficulties can actually be traced back to conflicting intimacy needs, is there anything you can do about it?

Perhaps one of the most intriguing findings in adult attachment research is that attachment styles are stable but plastic. This means that they tend to stay consistent over time, but they can also change. Up to now, we've described in detail what happens in anxious-avoidant relationships when left to run their usual course. Here we want to offer these couples a chance to work together to become more secure.

Attachment research shows that people tend to become more secure when they are in a relationship with someone secure. But there is also hope for a couple's future when neither partner is secure. Studies have found that security "priming"—reminding people of security-enhancing experiences they've had—can help them to create a greater sense of security. When people can recall a past relationship with a secure person or be inspired by a secure role model in their lives, they are often successful at adopting secure ways. As a person's attachment style gradually changes toward greater security, he or she behaves more constructively in relationships and even enjoys better mental and physical health. And if both partners are able to do so—the results can be remarkable.

IDENTIFYING YOUR INTEGRATED SECURE ROLE MODEL

Priming for security can be as simple as thinking about secure people around you and how they behave in their relationships. To find such a role model, mentally review the various people in your life, past and present. The secure presence can be someone close like a parent or a sibling, or it may be someone you know more casually from work or through friends. What's important is that this person has a secure attachment style and a secure way of dealing with people. Once you've come up with one or more such people, try to conjure specific images and recollections of the way they interact in the world: the kinds of things they say, how they act in different situations, what they choose to ignore and what they respond to, the way they behave when their partner is feeling down, and their general outlook on life and relationships. For example:

> *"Once when I disagreed with my manager, I came out very strongly against him. He showed a genuine interest in what I had to say and created a dialogue with me instead of a dueling match."*

"My best friend, Jon, and his wife, Laura, are always encouraging each other to do the things that they are passionate about. When Laura decided to leave her law firm and go into social work, Jon was the first to give her his blessing, even though it meant a serious financial cutback."

Your Relationship with Your Pet as a Secure Role Model?

•

Suzanne Phillips, coauthor of the book *Healing Together*, describes our connection with our pets as a source of inspiration for our romantic relationships. In her writing, she points out that we tend to perceive our pets as selfless and loving despite their many misdemeanors: They wake us up at night, destroy our valuables, and demand our undivided attention, yet we tend to overlook these behaviors and feel positively toward them. In fact, our connection with our pets is an excellent example of a secure presence in our lives. We can tap into our attitudes toward our pets as a secure resource within us—we don't assume our pets are doing things purposely to hurt us, we don't hold grudges even when they eat something they shouldn't or make a mess, we still greet them warmly when we come home (even after a rough day at the office), and we stick by them no matter what.

Go over all the secure examples that you've come up with and summarize the characteristics that you would like to adopt. This will become your integrated secure role model. This is what you want to strive for.

RESHAPING YOUR WORKING MODELS

In attachment research, "working model" is a phrase that describes our basic belief system when it comes to romantic relationships—what gets you going, what shuts you down, your attitudes and expectations. In short, what makes you tick in relationships. It is helpful to understand the ins and outs of your working model as a first step toward identifying patterns of thoughts, feelings, and actions that stand in the way of your becoming more secure.

Creating Your Relationship Inventory

The first order of business, therefore, is to become aware of the working model that governs your relationship behavior. Although you might have a good idea about your attachment style from what you've read so far, the relationship inventory will help you see more clearly how your attachment style affects your day-to-day thoughts, feelings, and behaviors in romantic situations.

The inventory will walk you through your past and present relationships from an attachment perspective. Research into the molecular mechanism of memory and learning reveals that whenever we recall a scene—or retrieve a certain memory to our conscious mind—we disrupt it, and by doing so, we alter it forever. Our memories are not like old books in the library, lying there dusty and unchanged; they are rather like a living, breathing entity. What we remember today of our past is in fact a product of editing and reshaping that occurs over the years whenever we recall that particular memory. In other words, our current experiences shape our view of our past ones. By creating your own attachment inventory, you reexamine your recollections of past relationship experiences from a fresh new perspective. Viewing them through an attachment lens will allow you to change some unhelpful beliefs that rely on those particular memories, and by so doing reshape your working model into a more secure one.

On pages 168–169 is the attachment relationship inventory. Taking the inventory is a task that should be done alone. Make sure to set aside enough quiet time to work on it thoroughly, so you really get a complete and accurate picture of yourself from an attachment perspective. Start by listing, in the left-hand column (1), the names of all your romantic partners, past and present. These can include people you've dated briefly. We suggest working vertically, one column at a time. Completing the inventory vertically encourages you to focus less on each particular scenario and to achieve an integrated picture of your working model across relationships. The more information you gather, the better. In column 2, write what you remember about the relationship: what it was like and what things stand out most when you try to recall your time together. Once you write down your general recollections of the relationship, column 3 allows you to take a closer look and identify specific scenarios that contribute to activation/deactivation of your attachment system. Column 4 asks how you responded to these situations: What did you do? What were you thinking? How did you feel? The lists below the inventory are provided to help you recall these reactions.

Column 5 is a crucial next step. You will need to reassess these experiences from an attachment perspective to gain insight into the issues that affected your relationships. What attachment issues underlie your reactions: Protest behavior? Deactivation? Refer to the lists as a guide. In column 6, you're asked to consider ways in which your reaction—now translated into attachment principles—hurts you and gets in the way of your happiness. Finally, column 7 prompts you to consider new, secure ways of handling these situations using a security-enhancing role model in your life and the secure principles we outline in this book (and in the box on page 174).

RELATIONSHIP INVENTORY

1. Name of partner	2. What is/was the relationship like? What recurrent patterns can you recall?	3. Situation that triggered activation or deactivation of attachment system	4. My reaction (thoughts, feelings, actions)

5. Insecure attachment working models and principles	6. How I lose out by succumbing to these working models/ principles	7. Identify a secure role model who is relevant to this situation *and* secure principles to adopt. How is s/he relevant?

Common *Anxious* Thoughts, Emotions, and Reactions

•

Thoughts

- Mind reading: That's it, I know s/he's leaving me.
- I'll never find anyone else.
- I knew this was too good to last.
- All-or-nothing thinking: I've ruined everything, there's nothing I can do to mend the situation.
- S/he can't treat me this way! I'll show him/her!
- I knew something would go wrong; nothing ever works out right for me.
- I have to talk to or see him/her right now.
- S/he'd better come crawling back to beg my forgiveness, otherwise s/he can forget about me forever.
- Maybe if I look drop-dead gorgeous or act seductive, things will work out.
- S/he is so amazing, why would s/he want to be with me anyway?
- Remembering all the good things your partner ever did and said after calming down from a fight.
- Recalling only the bad things your partner has ever done when you're fighting.

Emotions

- Sad
- Angry
- Fearful
- Resentful
- Frustrated
- Depressed

- Hopeless
- Despairing
- Jealous
- Hostile
- Vengeful
- Guilty
- Self-loathing
- Restless
- Uneasy
- Humiliated
- Hate-filled
- Uncertain
- Agitated
- Rejected
- Unloved
- Lonely
- Misunderstood
- Unappreciated

Actions

- Act out.
- Attempt to reestablish contact at any cost.
- Pick a fight.
- Wait for them to make the first reconciliation move.
- Threaten to leave.
- Act hostile—roll your eyes, look disdainful.
- Try to make him/her feel jealous.
- Act busy or unapproachable.
- Withdraw—stop talking to your partner or turn away from him/her physically.
- Act manipulatively.

Common *Avoidant* Thoughts, Emotions, and Reactions

•

Thoughts

- All-or-nothing thinking: I knew s/he wasn't right for me, this proves it!
- Overgeneralizing: I knew I wasn't made to be in a close relationship.
- S/he's taking over my life, I can't take it!
- Now I have to do everything his/her way; the price is too high.
- I need to get out of here, I feel suffocated.
- If s/he was "the one" this kind of thing wouldn't happen.
- When I was with (phantom X) this wouldn't have happened.
- Malicious intent: S/he's really out to annoy me, it's so obvious. . . .
- S/he just wants to tie me down, this isn't true love.
- Fantasize about having sex with other people.
- I'll be better off on my own.
- Ugh, s/he's so needy! It's pathetic.

Emotions

- Withdrawn
- Misunderstood
- Frustrated
- Resentful
- Angry
- Hostile
- Pressured
- Aloof
- Unappreciated
- Empty

- Deceived
- Tense
- Hate-filled
- Self-righteous
- Contemptuous
- Despairing
- Scornful
- Restless
- Distrustful

Actions

- Act out.
- Get up and leave.
- Belittle your partner.
- Act hostile, look disdainful.
- Make critical remarks.
- Withdraw mentally or physically.
- Minimize physical contact.
- Keep emotional sharing to a minimum.
- Stop listening to your partner. Ignore him/her.

Possible Attachment Principles at Play

•

Anxious

- Protest behavior
- Activating strategies—any thought, feeling, or behavior that will result in an increased desire to reconnect
- Putting your partner on a pedestal
- Feeling small and inferior in comparison to your partner

- Seeing/remembering only the best in your partner after a fight (while forgetting his/her negative side)
- Mistaking an activated attachment system for love
- Living in the danger zone (see chart on page 83)
- Living on an emotional roller coaster—getting addicted to the highs and the lows

Avoidant

- Deactivating strategies
- Mistaking self-reliance for independence
- Inflating your own importance and self-esteem while putting your partner down
- Seeing only the negative in your partner and ignoring the positive
- Assuming malicious intent in your partner's actions
- Disregarding your partner's emotional cues
- Yearning for the phantom ex
- Fantasizing about "the one"
- Repressing loving feelings and emotions

Examples of Secure Principles

·

- Be available.
- Don't interfere.
- Act encouragingly.
- Communicate effectively.

- Don't play games.
- View yourself as responsible for your partner's well-being.
- Wear your heart on your sleeve—be courageous and honest in your interactions.
- Maintain focus on the problem at hand.
- Don't make generalizations during conflict.
- Douse the flame before it becomes a forest fire—attend to your partner's upsets before they escalate.

It sometimes may be helpful to go over the inventory with an attachment-designated person (ADP), such as a family member, a close friend, or a therapist. Being able to turn to someone who is familiar with your patterns when your system goes into overdrive and your judgment is clouded by activation/deactivation can give you a new and different perspective. Your ADP can remind you of your destructive attachment tendencies and help you move toward a more secure emotional head space before you act out and hurt the relationship.

If you've completed the relationship inventory you have identified your working model and the ways in which it may interfere with your happiness and productivity. You've probably spotted the recurrent patterns in your relationships and the way in which you and your partners (past or present) tick each other off. You can even summarize these for yourself.

My Working Model—Summarizing the Inventory

Can you identify particular situations that are prone to activate (if you are anxious) or deactivate (if you are avoidant) your attachment system across relationships?

- _____
- _____
- _____

Can you detect ways in which an inefficient working model has prevented you from achieving more security?

- _____
- _____
- _____

What are the main attachment principles at play in your relationships?

- _____
- _____
- _____

Go back to your inventory and ask yourself how the secure role models (or integrated secure role model) can shed new light on the relationship issues you are/were dealing with.

- What would they do if they were in such a situation?
- Which point of view would they bring to the table?
- What would they tell you if they knew you were dealing with this issue?
- How is your experience with them relevant to the situation?

The answer to these questions will help you complete the last—and crucial—column of the inventory.

The two examples below will allow you to better understand how this approach can work and how to use the inventory.

THE TEXT MESSAGE
THAT SAVED THE DAY

When we interviewed Georgia and Henry for the book, they were constantly quarreling. According to Henry, nothing he ever did was good enough for Georgia, and he was always being judged and criticized. Georgia, for her part, believed that the onus of the marriage was on her. She had to run after Henry to make even simple plans and was always the one to initiate everything—from buying a birthday present for his mother to deciding which apartment to rent. She felt very alone in the partnership. When we encouraged Georgia to start monitoring her working model, which was clearly anxious, she came up with a particular situation that occurred frequently and always upset her. Henry never had time to talk to her during the workday. She would call and leave a message, but he would rarely get back to her. Georgia's inventory included the following entry:

1. Name	2. What is/was the relationship like? What recurrent patterns can you recall?	3. Situation that triggered activation or deactivation of attachment system	4. My reaction (thoughts, feelings, actions)
Henry	I feel that I'm alone and uncared for in this relationship. I'm tired of doing most of the relationship work on my own.	Henry not returning calls throughout the workday.	Feel anxious and restless. Wonder if I've done something to anger Henry. Stomach in a knot. Call incessantly or force myself to wait for him to call me. Act hostile when he phones.

5. Insecure attachment working models and principles	6. How I lose out by succumbing to these working models/ principles	7. Identify a secure role model who is relevant to this situation *and* secure principles to adopt. How is s/he relevant?
Activation: The feeling of anxiety and unrest and the need to talk to Henry RIGHT NOW are my attachment system's way of getting me to remain close to Henry. *Protest Behavior:* Acting hostile when Henry calls is my way of getting Henry to really pay attention to me and try to make up with me.	Instead of connecting with Henry, I end up fighting with him. Also, worrying about his availability hurts my concentration at work—and this happens even though I know he loves me!	Debbie, my therapist, who was a great secure presence in my life, told me to call her whenever I was upset. She said, "Georgia, I'd rather spend ten minutes on the phone with you than have you go upset all day." I never ended up having to call her. It was her availability that was important. I think I don't really need to talk to Henry so many times. My real need is to know that he's available and connected. By calling Henry many times I am also violating the secure base rule of noninterference.

Henry, who has an avoidant attachment style, was busy at work with patients, and would get frustrated by Georgia's incoming calls and text messages. When he eventually returned her calls, the dialogue would start off on a sour note that would affect the entire course of the conversation. This is what part of his inventory looked like:

1. Name	2. What is/was the relationship like? What recurrent patterns can you recall?	3. Situation that triggered activation or deactivation of attachment system	4. My reaction (thoughts, feelings, actions)
Georgia	There is never peace and quiet in our relationship. Georgia is very demanding of attention.	Georgia's repeated phone calls and text messages when I'm busy at work.	Feel frustrated. Get angry thinking about how needy Georgia is. Turn off my cell phone or answer her calls curtly and irritably.

5. Insecure attachment working models and principles	6. How I lose out by succumbing to these working models/ principles	7. Identify a secure role model who is relevant to this situation *and* secure principles to adopt. How is s/he relevant?
Deactivation: View Georgia as needy and overdependent. Forget that she's not out to get me and that she loves me and cares about me. *Withdrawal:* I distance myself by turning off the phone or acting hostile when we eventually talk.	When I get home Georgia is upset and I feel guilty. Also, often she's calling for a good reason (like which restaurant I'd like her to reserve for tonight) and I lose out by ignoring her.	My boss and his wife always check in with each other. They are this power couple at the hospital—both division chiefs. She even calls to make sure his schedule leaves him enough time for exercise. They really help each other succeed. I'm also violating the secure base rule of "availability." I need to find a way to be available for Georgia when she needs me.

Once both Georgia and Henry analyzed their working models, they started viewing their situation differently. Henry realized that by ignoring his wife's needs and ridiculing her dependency, he was only making matters worse and causing unhappiness in the relationship. Georgia realized that by using protest behavior she was actually distancing Henry instead of making him want to be there for her, as she assumed. When they sat down and talked about this recurrent issue, they were both better prepared. Henry said that although he did think about her during the day, he was so busy that he just didn't have time to stop and call. It was reassuring for Georgia to hear that Henry often thought about her when they were apart. She also understood his busy schedule. She just knew that she needed to feel more connected throughout the day.

Then they found a cool solution: Henry asked if it would be okay to send her a prewritten text message whenever he thought about her. It would only take a moment of his time but would reduce Georgia's worry greatly. This solution worked wonders for their relationship. For Georgia, receiving a "thinking of you" message enabled her to calm down and concentrate better at work, and Henry felt less resentful once he realized that Georgia wasn't out to destroy his career by endless nagging. In fact, by invoking his boss's special relationship with his wife, he could see how a secure base could help advance his career. At night when they met, the tension was gone and the neediness and hostility were no longer there.

THE TOOTHPASTE INCIDENT

Sam really wanted Grace to move in with him when she moved to New York City. They'd been together for over two years and he thought that it would be nice to take their relationship to a higher level. Besides, they were staying at each other's place all the time and think of the rent they would save! Grace preferred not to move into Sam's apartment. She wanted to rent a bigger place instead, where they could both start on equal footing. But Sam refused; he loved his little apartment and saw no reason to spend money when he owned a place of his own. He was sure that they could make it work. He did have some hesitations, though. He'd never lived with anyone before and he was very set in his ways. But over the years, he'd also felt the loneliness that comes with self-sufficiency and wanted something more. Then when Grace moved in, Sam started to feel the pressure mounting. Sometimes he felt he was going to suffocate. Her things were everywhere. He felt that he was losing his quiet sanctuary, and quite literally that his home had been invaded. Finally one day he lost it—it was about the toothpaste. Grace always squeezed the toothpaste from the middle, while he made sure to carefully squeeze it from the bottom up. When he noticed the distorted toothpaste tube, he became furious and told Grace that she was sloppy and careless. Grace was caught off guard; she'd been trying very hard to make her presence in the apartment unobtrusive, and an attack was the last thing she expected.

A while later, after thinking things over, Sam made the following revelations:

1. Name	2. What is/was the relationship like? What recurrent patterns can you recall?	3. Situation that triggered activation or deactivation of attachment system	4. My reaction (thoughts, feelings, actions)
Grace	I thought we got along well, now I'm not so sure anymore. Maybe I'm not cut out for living with someone else.	Grace moving into my place, making changes and doing things her own way—the toothpaste business being the last straw.	Get upset and angry. Think moving in with Grace was all a big mistake—I feel like a stranger in my own home. I'm trapped. Find fault with everything Grace does. Think how incapable she is. Sulk a lot.

5. Insecure attachment working models and principles	6. How I lose out by succumbing to these working models/principles	7. Identify a secure role model who is relevant to this situation *and* secure principles to adopt. How is s/he relevant?
Deactivation: View Grace as incompetent and intruding. Repress loving feelings—forget how important it was for me to move in together and how unhappy and lonely I've been in the past.	I want her to do everything my way in the house, which makes her tense, and the tension is contagious. I'm risking my relationship with Grace and hurting the only partner I've ever really cared about. Living alone will be like going back to square one. I was lonely and unhappy. That's why I went to therapy. It was through my work in therapy that I was able to get into this relationship.	My therapist said to just give it time, not to come out with any grand statements about not being cut out to live with someone. It's an adjustment. My best friend has been living with his partner for more than a year now. They go food shopping together and do other household chores in tandem. I was very jealous of them before Grace moved in with me. I'm violating the secure base rule of noninterference. This place is new for her. I need to be supportive and not make her feel bad.

And this is what Grace's entry looked like:

1. Name	2. What is/was the relationship like? What recurrent patterns can you recall?	3. Situation that triggered activation or deactivation of. attachment system	4. My reaction (thoughts, feelings, actions)
Sam	I don't know what's happened lately. We were getting along so well, but since I moved in he's been acting distant and mean. I knew we should have gotten a place that was new for us both.	Living together and being constantly criticized.	I feel that everything I do is wrong. I'm convinced he doesn't love me anymore. Why did I move in with him? I've been reduced to acting like a guest in my own home. Now I'm trapped. I feel very inadequate. Am I really such a slob? I think we won't be able to survive this. We'll probably break up soon.

After doing his inventory, Sam realized that years of living alone and believing in his own self-sufficiency were now being challenged head-on. He was overwhelmed and discussed his new

5. Insecure attachment working models and principles	6. How I lose out by succumbing to these working models/principles	7. Identify a secure role model who is relevant to this situation *and* secure principles to adopt. How is s/he relevant?
Generalizing a specific scenario onto the entire relationship. Putting myself down. Jumping to—"the relationship is over"—conclusion. Being immersed in negative memories and emotions.	Again I will create a self-fulfilling prophecy. I will act hostile and be upset and unpleasant until the relationship will really be over. I can't think about a specific solution when I see things so extremely.	My sister made a good point: She said that Sam lives and works from home and I'm around a lot. Maybe it's too much all at once. It won't hurt to have a buffer zone to gradually ease us into living together. People need time to adjust. She said that when she first moved in with her now husband, they also went through a period of adjustment. I'm violating the secure base rule of supportiveness: I need to be more supportive. This is harder for him than it is for me.

understanding with Grace. Grace realized that she was threatened by the fact that Sam was having difficulty adjusting to her presence. She also saw how she was interpreting the situation and reacting to it in a way that was harming the relationship. She liked her sister's idea of finding a buffer zone. Since Grace's close friend was going out of town for six months, Grace brought up the idea of subletting her friend's studio apartment for a while so she would have a place of her own to do her art work and other hobbies without worrying about Sam's reaction. Sam was surprised at her suggestion. Knowing that Grace now had an alternative made a huge difference to him. All at once he no longer felt suffocated and was less bothered by the changes she made. After six months, during which time Grace barely ever actually stayed at her sublet apartment, she didn't bother to look for another sublet—Sam and she had adjusted to living together.

MAKE BECOMING SECURE AN ONGOING GROWTH PROCESS

Remember that attachment styles are stable and plastic—becoming more secure is an ongoing process. Whenever a new concern, dissatisfaction, or conflict occurs, enter the new information. This will help in your quest to break your insecure patterns. But moving toward security is not only about tackling problems in your relationship; it's also about having fun together. Find ways to enjoy your time together as a couple—a walk in the park, a movie and dinner, watching a TV show that you both like—and make time to be physically close. Shedding your insecure working model will do wonders for your ability to function in the world at large. Dr. Sue Johnson, the founder of Emotionally Focused Therapy (EFT) has demonstrated through her clinical work and writings that creating true security in the relationship and recognizing that you are emotionally dependent on your partner on every level is the best way to improve your romantic bond. Another pioneer in the field of applied attachment is Dr. Dan Siegel, who in his numerous books (*The Developing Mind, Parenting from the Inside Out,* and *Mindsight,* to name just a few), helps people become more secure. Using a unique technique, he teaches people with insecure attachments how to narrate their past history in a secure fashion. The ability to recall your own childhood memories of your relationships with your primary caregivers in a more coherent manner has remarkable effects; it helps you become a better, more reflective parent and improves other areas of your life.

When you build a secure relationship, both individuals win: If you are the anxious partner, you get the closeness you crave, and if you're the avoidant partner, you'll enjoy much more of the independence you need.

WHAT IF THE GOAL OF SECURITY IS NOT REACHED?

What happens if despite your efforts to move your relationship away from "the trap" and the vicious insecure cycle, you are unable to do so? This can happen either because there is no genuine wish to change on the part of one or both partners or your attempts fail. We believe that when people are in an anxious-avoidant relationship, especially when they are unable to move to greater security, these discrepancies will always be a part of their lives and will never completely disappear. But we also strongly believe that knowledge is power. And it can be very valuable to know that your ongoing struggles as a couple are not because either of you is crazy, but rather because your relationship has a built-in clash that is not going to go away.

One of the most important benefits of this insight has to do with your self-perception. Intimacy clashes are very destructive for the non-avoidant partner, who is constantly being pushed away by the avoidant partner. We can see this happening in the examples we cite throughout the book, in behaviors such as maintaining a high degree of secrecy and then blaming the other person of being jealous and needy, in preferring separate beds, and in finding ways to spend less time together. If you are with an avoidant partner, you are constantly being rejected and rebuffed. After experiencing these distancing strategies for a while, you start to blame yourself. You may believe that if your partner was with someone else, s/he'd act differently; that with another s/he'd surely want to be closer than with you. You begin to feel unattractive and inadequate.

Understanding that your continual arguments actually have a hidden subtext to them—that they genuinely are irresolvable—changes your perception of your own role dramatically. Once you understand that your partner will always find areas of contention as a way of maintaining distance and that s/he will always need to withdraw, no matter whom s/he is with—you will no longer blame yourself for the relationship problems.

At least on the surface, the avoidant partner gets hurt less, because withdrawal is a one-sided move that doesn't necessitate cooperation from your partner. However, although seemingly unperturbed, an important lesson to be learned is that indifference does not connote security. Avoidants need to actively suppress their attachment needs, but they tend to report being less happy in relationships. Still, they often blame their unhappiness on their partner.

But how do people live with this understanding?

When we interviewed Alana, she told us about her relationship with her ex-husband, Stan. She recounted how they were able to find some stability in the relationship as long as Stan worked most of the time, and on weekends they did various separate chores and spent very little down time together. But things would become more difficult whenever Alana would ask him to go on a romantic getaway in the hope that it would bring them closer. On these occasions, Stan would always find an excuse for not going. They used to have a ritual whereby Alana would tell her friends and coworkers that she and Stan were going away for the weekend; she would get excited, make plans, and start to pack. A few days later she would call them sounding defeated and worn out, to say that something came up at the last minute, and they never went. Once it was his work, another time he wasn't feeling well, and yet another time the car needed repairs. They'd have a huge fight and then things would calm down again—until the next time. For Alana, getting her hopes up, only to be disappointed again and again, was a painful experience.

Eventually Alana's relationship with Stan ended. She never really grasped that her fights with him were about something much more fundamental than whether to go on vacation (or even about romance, for that matter). Instead they were about a big barrier that he put up between them. And even if at some deep level she did understand, she wasn't able to truly accept this reality or live with it.

Other people do find a way to live in relative peace with colliding intimacy needs. How do they manage? They come to terms with the fact that when it comes to certain aspects of the relationship, things are not ever going to change. They understand that they can choose to live a Sisyphean life of ongoing disappointment and frustration, one in which they will continuously fight a losing battle. Or they can change their expectations. They learn to accept certain limitations and adopt a number of pragmatic life strategies:

- They admit to themselves that in certain areas, their mate is never going to be an active partner, and they stop urging him or her to change.
- They stop taking personal offense when their mate pushes them away and accept that this is simply his or her *nature*.
- They learn to do things on their own that they previously expected to do with their partner.
- They engage with like-minded friends in activities that their mate is unwilling to participate in.
- They learn to be thankful for what their mate *does* do and to overlook what he or she *does not* do.

We know countless people who, after having struggled with ongoing intimacy conflicts, finally make a shift in their mind-set and find a compromise that they are able to live with:

- **Doug, 53,** used to get furious at his wife on a daily basis when she came home hours later than expected. He finally decided to stop getting mad when she walked in and to greet her warmly instead. He made a conscious decision to make home into a place she would *want* to come home to instead of a battlefield.
- **Natalie, 38,** always dreamed of sharing her leisure time with her husband. After years of resentment and bitter

fights over his refusal to spend weekends together, she decided to change. Today she makes plans for herself. If he wants to join (as rarely happens), he's welcome aboard. But if not, it's "so long and see you later."

- **Janis, 43,** is married to Larry. Larry, who was married before, doesn't take an active role in raising their joint children. Janis has come to accept that when it comes to the kids (and several other areas of their life together), she is quite literally on her own. She no longer expects him to participate and no longer gets angry when he refuses to do so.

All these individuals share chronic, ongoing intimacy collisions with their partners. They have chosen to let go of the dream of being truly intimate with their partners and have found a way to live with limited togetherness. They compromise. But make no mistake: The compromise is in no way mutual; it is in fact wholly one-sided. Instead of engaging in endless conflict that results in nothing but frustration and disappointment, they have decided to change their expectations and reduce conflict to tolerable proportions.

DECIDING TO LET GO OF THE DREAM

Do we recommend taking this route? Our answer is—"It depends." If you're in an ongoing relationship riddled with intimacy clashes that you have not been able to resolve, and yet you want to remain in the bond for whatever reason, then yes, this is the only way to live in relative peace. Your satisfaction level in the relationship will be lower than that of people who don't experience such battles. But it will also be higher than that of people who choose to relive these fights day in and day out without ever accepting that they are about fundamental differences that aren't going to go away.

If, however, you're in a relatively new or uncommitted relationship and are already experiencing a lot of intimacy collisions, we advise you to think long and hard about whether you want to make so many concessions in order to be with this person. There is a major difference between couples who are dealing with non-attachment-related issues and those who are engaged in intimacy struggles. While the first couples want to find a common ground and reach a resolution that will bring them closer together, the latter either engage in ongoing, irreconcilable fights or one of the two is forced to compromise unilaterally in areas that are near and dear to him or her.

But there's more. This attachment collision can go from bad to worse. The next chapter depicts how intimacy clashes can get out of hand, what it takes to recognize the situation, and most important, how to leave it behind.

10

When Abnormal Becomes the Norm: An Attachment Guide to Breaking Up

C lay and Tom were enjoying a romantic dinner on their anniversary. Clay was gazing lovingly at Tom, when out of nowhere Tom snapped: "What the hell are you staring at? Stop staring, it's really annoying." Clay wanted to get up and leave but restrained himself. He said nothing, and they finished their dinner in silence.

Throughout their hiking trip in Guatemala, instead of walking side by side and sharing the adventure, Gary would walk ahead of Sue, occasionally making snide comments about how lazy and incompetent she was for walking so slowly.

After Pat finished giving her husband the "no reciprocation" sexual treat he asked for, he said, "That was awesome—and the greatest thing about it was that it could have just been anyone, a complete stranger. That's hot." Pat felt as though she'd been punched in the stomach.

In the previous chapter, we discussed problems arising from the anxious-avoidant clash and possible ways to resolve these issues. In some cases, however, even repeated efforts to improve the situation fail, and the interaction between these two attachment styles can become truly harmful. Unfortunately, in these cases, anxious and avoidant people can bring out the worst in each other. "Abnormal" becomes the norm.

A common view is that only masochistic, "pathetic" people would tolerate such bad treatment, and that if they are willing to put up with it instead of leaving, well, maybe they deserve it! Others believe that these people are reliving troubled childhood experiences in their adult life. The story of Marsha and Craig contradicts these typical assumptions. We met 31-year-old Marsha in the process of conducting interviews for this book. She was very open and forthcoming in recounting her story to us, and had no qualms about revealing very intimate and often hurtful moments in her life. She told us she wanted her story to be told in order to help other women who might find themselves in similar situations. She wanted them to know it was possible to get out of a destructive relationship and find happiness elsewhere. Marsha came from a loving, caring family, and after her relationship with Craig, she went on to meet an adoring man who treated her very well. The only "fault" we could find with Marsha was that she was anxious and Craig was avoidant. As we've discussed in chapter 5, there seems to be a gravitational pull between anxious and avoidant individuals, and once they become attached, it's very hard for them to let go. Marsha's story demonstrates what transpires in an extreme anxious-avoidant match and the mental struggle involved in ending it.

Though disturbing, Marsha's story ends on a hopeful note. We've included it for three reasons: to illustrate the power of the attachment process, to show that even emotionally healthy individuals can become entangled in a destructive situation, and to let people in those relationships know that they can find a better life for themselves if they muster the strength to leave.

MARSHA'S STORY

I met Craig when I was in college. He was cute and sporty, and I admired the way he looked. Plus, he was a tutor in physics, my major, doing work that seemed far more advanced than mine, so I thought he was brilliant. From the beginning, however, there were things about his behavior that confused and upset me.

When he first asked me out, I showed up for what I assumed was a date, only to discover it was a group event with a bunch of his friends. Although I knew that any woman would have understood his invitation the same way, I gave him the benefit of the doubt, allowing for the possibility that I'd misread him. Soon after that, he asked to go out with me alone, so I chalked up the first "date" to a misunderstanding.

A month later, I thought I'd surprise Craig by showing up to cheer him on at his track team practice. Not only did he not thank me for my support, he ignored me completely. He was with his friends and didn't even say hello. What could I do but conclude that he was ashamed of me?

Afterward, I confronted Craig about his behavior. He said, "Marsha, when we're in the company of other people, I don't

197

think they need to know we're a couple." His words made me furious and reduced me to tears. But then he hugged and kissed me, and I made up with him. Soon, despite Craig not acknowledging our relationship in public, it became apparent that we were indeed a couple.

Unfortunately, it wasn't the last time I discovered that we weren't on the same page. We'd been dating for several months, and to my mind our relationship was progressing nicely. So to make things clearer, I told my old boyfriend—whom I'd still meet on occasion—that I couldn't see him anymore. When I mentioned this to Craig, his response caught me off guard. "Why did you tell your ex that? It's still very early and this might not lead to anything!"

After a couple more months of seeing each other, Craig and I finally seemed to be in sync. He was moving into a one-bedroom apartment and suggested I move in with him. I liked it that he was making a commitment, and agreed. It seemed perfectly natural to everyone; Craig was a great guy and he made a good impression. People who knew him superficially thought he was really nice. The truth, however, was that my life with Craig was becoming an emotional roller coaster and I'd find myself in tears on a daily basis.

For one thing, Craig was always comparing me with his exgirlfriend Ginger. According to Craig, she was perfect—smart, beautiful, interesting, and sophisticated. The fact that they still kept in touch was extremely difficult for me and made me feel unsure of myself. While he was quick to build up Ginger, he was just as quick to belittle me, especially when it came to my intellectual abilities. It killed me that he thought that I was in some way slow. But I knew I was bright—after all, I was a student at an Ivy League university—so I let it go.

My confidence in my appearance was another story. I felt insecure about my looks, and it didn't help when Craig would zoom in on some feature—a bit of cellulite, for example—and go on about it for weeks. The first time he saw me naked in the shower he commented that I looked "like a midget with huge boobs." I took his disparaging remarks to heart, and at times would even put myself down. Once, after I'd eaten too much and was feeling fat, I asked him why he'd ever want to have sex with someone so disgusting. Now most boyfriends—indeed, most people—would respond to such a horrible moment of self-deprecation with something encouraging like, "Marsha, how could you say such a thing? You're gorgeous!"

But Craig simply replied, "You're what there is right now." It didn't even occur to him that his words might be offensive—as far as he was concerned, he was just making an observation.

I did try talking to him about how hurtful he could be, a few times going so far as to say that he seemed emotionally handicapped in some way. But my words would go in one ear and out the other. There were occasions I'd swear to myself that I couldn't take his behavior anymore, and I'd work up the nerve to say I was breaking up with him. But I was never able to follow through. He'd tell me that he loved me and I'd let him convince me that we should be together.

Did he love me? Maybe. He'd tell me so almost every day. I'd justify his behavior, convincing myself that he wasn't to blame, that he was brought up without an example of a healthy relationship. His father was very domineering and treated his mother badly. I became adept at rationalizing that he "just didn't know any better." If his behavior was learned, I could hope, think, possibly even expect, that he could unlearn it and change.

Attached

My denial required me to put up with a lot. Like his father, Craig was very forceful. It was all about *him*. We always did what he wanted; his opinions mattered more—in everything. He selected the movies we would see and planned what I would cook. Even though he knew that décor is very important to me, he decided we had to have a poster of Shaquille O'Neal in the living room. The living room!

Because I was so deeply ashamed of the way Craig treated me—of the way I let him treat me—I never met my friends in his presence. Time with his friends was bad enough. I can be quite shy, and once, when we were out with some people he knew, I was trying to break into the conversation with an opinion. He interrupted the speaker: "Hey, listen up, my 'genius' girlfriend wants to say something." Another time, at the beach, I asked him for a towel and he shouted, "Dry yourself in the sun!" in front of everyone. These were just two instances. There were many, many others. I kept asking him not to speak to me that way, but eventually I gave up.

The one aspect of our relationship that made things bearable—and allowed me to stay with him for so long—was that, despite his words, Craig was very affectionate. We hugged a lot and would fall asleep cuddling. The affection allowed me to pretend I was satisfied with our sex life. Craig was the least sexual boyfriend I ever had, and the comfort of the cuddling would reduce the pain of feeling rejected.

In my mind, I tried to compensate, but as time went on my thinking became more and more distorted. I'd say to myself, "No one has a perfect relationship, you have to compromise on something—if that's the case, I might as well be with Craig." Since we'd

200

been together for several years, I "reasoned" that I should stop wasting time and get married. Even after the terribly inappropriate comments he made when I suggested the idea to him, including, "But that means I'll never sleep with a woman in her twenties again!" I still wanted to marry him.

Marriage was the one decision that I pressured Craig into. As soon as he agreed, I knew it was a mistake. That was evident from the word "go." The ring he bought was unimpressive and the stones kept falling out. What more of an omen did I need?

Our honeymoon in Paris was awful. We were together all the time and I felt literally shackled to Craig. We had plenty of time to enjoy ourselves, but Craig turned everything into a problem. He complained about the service at the hotel and went ballistic when I accidentally got us on the wrong metro line. That was a white-light moment for me. When Craig started swearing at me, I realized that I was powerless to change him. When we finally got home and my family asked me about the honeymoon, I didn't have the courage to tell them it was a disaster. I said, "It was nice," in a pathetically feeble tone. What a miserable way to describe one's honeymoon.

Though I felt trapped, I still couldn't extract myself from the nightmare. Time after time when I mustered the courage to leave, Craig would convince me to stay. I began to fantasize that he would fall in love with someone else and leave, because I was afraid I'd never have the strength to leave him first. Luckily Craig found the strength. When I told him I wanted a divorce, for the umpteenth time, he again begged me to stay, but this time he promised that if I ever asked again, he wouldn't talk me out of it. I'm grateful that he kept his word. The next time things got unbearable, I told him

I wanted out, and he said, "Okay!" We'd signed a contract to buy an apartment together and lost $10,000 for pulling out of the deal, but looking back, it was the best money I ever spent.

The divorce was relatively quick and easy. We stayed in touch afterward. Once I wasn't tied to him any longer, it was actually fun spending time with him—in small doses. He was interesting, affectionate, and charming. When he became hurtful, I would just get up and leave.

Fortunately, Marsha went on to meet someone with whom she has a happy life. While with her new partner, she was able to change her job to one more rewarding and to develop a new hobby. She's never again experienced the emotional turmoil that she felt with Craig.

OPPOSING FORCES

Marsha and Craig's story exemplifies how bad an anxious-avoidant trap can become. Craig didn't feel comfortable with too much intimacy, so he missed no opportunity to put up emotional barriers between himself and Marsha—creating uncertainty at the beginning of their relationship, keeping their status unclear, having to be "pushed" into marriage, belittling her, avoiding sex, and using numerous other deactivating strategies. Clearly he possesses an avoidant attachment style. Marsha has an anxious attachment style. She longed to be close to Craig, she was the driving force behind their marriage, and she was preoccupied with the relationship— initially she cried every day because of his behavior, a form of preoccupation, and later she constantly thought of divorce, another way to focus on the relationship. In a typically anxious manner, she fluctuated from highs to lows, depending on the signals from Craig, and resorted to protest behavior (threatening to leave but never actually following through). Her attachment system remained chronically activated, at least during the first few years—before she became indifferent to him.

It is evident that each side had very different needs in the relationship, resulting in a continuous clash. Craig's need was to keep his distance and Marsha's was to get closer. Craig's inflated self-esteem (an avoidant characteristic) fed off Marsha's increasing self-doubt (an anxious characteristic). But there were also endearing moments between them that made it difficult for her to leave. For example, Craig sometimes knew how to be very affectionate and loving and how to soothe Marsha when things got to be too much (even though usually they got to be too much because of him!). Yet every instance of their closeness was followed by his distancing, which is typical of anxious-avoidant relationships.

A WORD ABOUT SEX

Note Marsha's statement that Craig was "the least sexual person I ever dated." Avoidants often use sex to distance themselves from their partner. It doesn't necessarily mean they will cheat on their partner, although studies have shown that they are more likely to do so than other attachment types. Phillip Shaver, in a study with then University of California–Davis graduate student Dory Schachner, found that of the three styles, avoidants would more readily make a pass at someone else's partner or respond to such a proposition.

But even when avoidants do stay faithful, they have other ways of using sex to push their partners away. While people with an anxious attachment style prefer strong emotional involvement during sex and enjoy the intimate aspects of lovemaking like kissing and caressing, avoidants have very different preferences. They might choose to focus only on the sexual act itself, forgoing holding and cuddling, or to put rules into place like "no kissing" in order to make sex feel less intimate. Others might have sex only rarely—or never—with their partner, or fantasize about others while doing so. (Long-term couples may use fantasy to spice up their sex life, but they do so as a way to get closer. With avoidants, fantasy is not part of a mutual adventure but rather a deactivating strategy to keep them isolated.) In fact, in a study of married and cohabiting couples, Canadian scientists Audrey Brassard and Yvan Lussier, along with Phillip Shaver, found that avoidant men and women had sex less with their partners than did people with other attachment styles.

Intriguingly, they also found that avoidant men and women were more likely to engage in less sex *if their partner had an anxious attachment style!* Researchers believe that in relationships like Marsha and Craig's, there is less lovemaking because the anxious partner wants a great deal of physical closeness and this in turn causes the avoidant partner to withdraw further. What better way to avoid intimacy than by reducing sex to a bare minimum?

What's more, it's been found that the anxious partner uses sex to achieve a sense of affirmation and as a barometer of attractiveness in the eyes of his/her mate. We can see that a clash is almost inevitable when the anxious person ascribes so much importance to the sexual experience and the avoidant person wants to avoid physical intimacy.

Of course there are anxious-avoidant relationships in which sex is not an issue. In that case, the emotional detachment will take on a different form.

LIFE IN THE INNER CIRCLE

But sex was hardly the main concern for Marsha during the time she was with Craig. It constituted just a fraction of the deactivating strategies used by Craig, day in, day out, whether with friends or in the privacy of their own home; his deactivation was relentless and never-ending. In short, Craig treated Marsha as if she were the enemy, in sharp contrast to the loving and caring persona he exhibited to the rest of the world ("Craig was a great guy and he made a good impression. People who knew him superficially thought he was really nice"). That dichotomy confused Marsha. Of all the people in the world, she was the one closest to him, and yet he treated her the worst. How could he be so nice toward everyone else and so mean to her? It didn't make sense, and she thought that if she could make him see that he was hurting her, then he could treat her as well as he treated everyone else.

Marsha wasn't aware that Craig treated her so badly not *in spite of* her being closest but *because* she was closest. She was now living within Craig's *inner circle*. When our partners join our inner circle, we become close to them in a way that we can be only with our closest relatives—our spouse and kids (and as children, with our parents and siblings). Unfortunately, life in the inner circle for an anxious-avoidant couple is not a bed of roses. Once Marsha crossed that line with Craig, she got too close for comfort and became the enemy. The more Marsha tried to get close, the more he tried to push her away. This is often what life can be like in the inner circle if you have an anxious attachment style and you are with someone avoidant.

SIGNS THAT YOU HAVE BECOME "THE ENEMY"

- You are ashamed to let friends and family know how your partner *really* treats you.
- You are surprised when people tell you how sweet, nice, or considerate your mate is.
- You listen in on your partner's conversations to learn what is really going on in his or her life.
- Your partner often consults other people, rather than you, about important issues.
- In an emergency, you feel uncertain that your partner will drop everything in order to be there for you.
- It is more important for your partner to make a good impression on strangers than on you.
- You're surprised when you see friends being treated considerately by their partners.
- You are the person most likely to be insulted or put down by your mate.
- Your emotional and physical health are low on your partner's priority list.

Do these statements apply to your situation? Chances are that if you're getting the cold shoulder, if your partner is much nicer to strangers and usually "pleads the fifth"—choosing not to talk to you—you've become the enemy. Your only crime has been to become too close to someone who can't tolerate it.

This is in very sharp contrast to life in the inner circle with someone secure.

THE INNER CIRCLE WHEN YOU'RE TREATED LIKE ROYALTY

- Your well-being comes second to none.
- You are confided in first.
- Your opinion matters most.
- You feel admired and protected.
- Your need for closeness is rewarded with even more closeness.

Many people in anxious-avoidant relationships think that the "royal inner circle" doesn't really exist, and that all people have the same inner-circle experience. They assume that other people are simply not being honest about what goes on behind closed doors. But we're here to tell you that it does exist and it's not even a rare occurrence. After all, secure people make up over 50 percent of the population and their inner circle *is* treated like royalty.

"Smoking Guns" in Marsha and Craig's Story
•

Within the first weeks and months (!) of Marsha and Craig's relationship, various signs—as obvious as smoking guns at a crime scene—could have alerted Marsha to the trap she was getting into:

- Craig ignored Marsha when she came to cheer him on during track practice.
- He tried to hide the fact that they were a couple.
- He was surprised that Marsha stopped seeing her ex-boyfriend (suggesting that he didn't value commitment himself).
- He made devaluing and degrading remarks about her.
- He compared her unfavorably to his "phantom ex," Ginger.
- He responded to Marsha's worries and self-doubts in a way that made her feel worse.
- Most important, in all of these actions, he conveyed a strong message that he was not able to properly take care of Marsha's emotional needs.

For more about smoking guns, see chapter 5.

ADMITTING THERE'S A PROBLEM

Many people who live in an avoidant-anxious trap have a hard time admitting to themselves and others that they are in a bad predicament. They'll admit that they're not completely satisfied with their relationship, then will qualify it by saying, "But who is? All couples fight, all couples get upset. How are we different from them?" They talk themselves into believing that their partner's behavior is not so bad. Others, like Marsha, are aware of their dire situation, but can't take the necessary steps to bail out. They might make an attempt, but get overwhelmed by the pain associated with leaving. Then they experience the *rebound effect.*

THE REBOUND EFFECT

Once you're convinced that you've become the enemy, why is it still so hard to walk away? First, because it is very painful. As painful as it is to be mistreated by your partner, severing an attachment bond is even more excruciating. You may understand rationally that you should leave, but your emotional brain may not yet be ready to make that move. The emotional circuits that make up our attachment system evolved to discourage us from being alone. One way to nudge us back to the safety of our lover's arms is to create the sensation of unmistakable pain when we find ourselves alone. Studies have found that the same areas in the brain that light up in imaging scans when we break a leg are activated when we split up with our mate. As part of a reaction to a breakup, our brain experiences the departure of an attachment figure in a similar way to that in which it registers physical pain.

But it's not just a feeling of pain that takes over. Other thought processes are also hijacked in the process. Once your attachment system becomes activated, another interesting phenomenon is triggered: You will get overwhelmed by positive memories of the few good times you had together and forget the multitude of bad experiences. You'll recall how sweet he or she was to you the other day when you were distressed and conveniently forget that he or she was the one to hurt you in the first place. An activated attachment system is immensely powerful. It is a very important reason why Marsha stayed as long as she did.

RETURNING TO THE SCENE OF THE CRIME

What happens when you do reunite with your partner after a breakup? Myron Hofer, a colleague of Amir's from Columbia University and a leading researcher in the field of the psychobiology of mother-infant attachment, describes a fascinating discovery in one of his studies. When rat pups are separated from their mothers, a number of physiological reactions occur: their activity level goes down, their heart rate goes down, and so does their growth hormone level. In Hofer's studies, he gradually replaced each maternal attribute with an artificial substitute: He first warmed the pups with a heating pad, then fed them so their stomachs would be full, and later patted them with a brush, imitating their mother's licking action. He found that each intervention helped with *one* aspect of their separation distress. Feeding the pups helped maintain their heart rate at a normal level, warming them helped keep their activity intact, and brushing them helped raise their growth hormone secretion.

But only one intervention alleviated all the symptoms at once, and that was the reunion with their mother.

For humans, the situation is very similar. When we break up with someone, our attachment system goes into overdrive, and just like the rat pups, we can think of nothing but getting back together with our loved one. The fact that one person can take away all our discomfort in a split second makes it very hard to resist the temptation to see him or her again. Just being in the same room is enough to entirely relieve the anxiety in a way that no other single friend or family member can.

For this simple reason, many individuals find it hard to follow through on their wish to break up, even after they've tried more than once to do it. It also explains why Marsha chose to maintain some contact with Craig, long after they separated. Anxious people may take a very long time to get over a bad attachment, and they don't get to decide how long it will take. Only when every single cell in their body is completely convinced that there is no chance that their partner will change or that they will ever reunite will they be able to deactivate and let go.

ESCAPE FROM ALCATRAZ

Even without knowing about the rebound effect, Marsha could see that she was in trouble. After all, she had experienced the rebound effect before. Marsha was afraid that she might have a change of heart again, and she was greatly relieved when Craig took matters into his own hands—standing by his word to leave, the next time she threatened him with divorce. The night she said she wanted out, everything happened very quickly. She packed a small bag and called her sister to pick her up right away. From an attachment perspective, this was a very well-planned departure.

Being near her sister in a familiar, nurturing environment helped with one aspect of her distressed attachment system; talking to her friends on the phone and getting their support was another; eating ice cream and chocolate, yet another. None of these comforts completely relieved her separation distress, and sometimes she lost sight of why she had needed to break up with Craig. Then her friends and family would remind her, sometimes on an hourly basis, why it was necessary.

WHEN DEACTIVATING STRATEGIES ARE A GOOD THING

Long before she actually made a break, Marsha had been unconsciously preparing her escape by beginning to deactivate her attachment system. After trying for years to make things work with Craig—by explaining her point of view, falling apart emotionally, and excusing his behavior—she finally gave up hope. In our interview, Marsha told us that whereas during the first few years she would find herself in tears on a daily basis, during the last year, she almost never cried. Emotionally, she was already starting to detach. She no longer believed that anything would change or, in fact, that Craig *could* change. She started to notice more and more of his faults and stopped concentrating on the occasional positive experience they shared. The process she went through was the same one that avoidant people engage in all the time: In order to avoid becoming too close, they focus on their partner's negative qualities and behaviors to keep their partner at bay. Marsha, although anxious, started to use deactivating strategies after having been burned emotionally by Craig countless times. Deactivating is a necessary process that must occur in order to get someone out of your (attachment) system. Starting this process while still with your partner, however, doesn't guarantee that you won't experience the rebound effect. Once your attachment system is reactivated as a result of separation, all bets are off. In Marsha's case, having started the deactivation process did help her get safely through the initial breakup phase and the eventual divorce.

Today Marsha is no longer in contact with Craig and they are not friends. Instead, she went on to find herself a real soul mate.

Surviving a Breakup

•

The following nine strategies, using attachment principles, will help you get through the painful experience of ending a relationship.

1. **Ask yourself what life is like for you in the "inner circle."** If you can't decide to break up, ask yourself whether you are treated like royalty or like the enemy. If you're the enemy, it's time to go.
2. **Build a support network *ahead of time*.** Start to open up to friends and family about what your relationship is *really* like. This will rekindle friendships you might have neglected due to shame or plain misery, and will also prepare them to help you when you make your move (see how in strategy 7).
3. **Find a comforting, supportive place to stay for the first few nights.** You'll need all the support you can get at first. The temptation to rebound is very strong. Parents, siblings, or your closest friends can help you control that urge.

4. **Get your attachment needs met in other ways.** Recruit support from the people closest to you and seek diversions like a massage, plenty of exercise, and comforting, healthy food. The more you are able to quiet down your attachment system, the less painful the separation will be.

5. **Don't be ashamed if you slip up and go back to "the scene of the crime."** Obviously you're better off not reestablishing contact with your ex, but if you end up doing so, don't beat yourself up. It is very important that you be compassionate with yourself. The worse you feel about yourself, the more you'll want to go back to the false safety of the bad relationship you were in. Your attachment system gets activated more when you feel bad about yourself and an activated attachment system means wanting to renew contact even more.

6. **If you're having a hard time, don't feel guilty. Remember, the pain is real!** Friends might urge you to forget about your ex, stop feeling sorry for yourself, and move on quickly. But we know that the pain you're feeling is real, so don't deny it. Instead, be kind to yourself and find ways to pamper your body and soul. You would if you had a broken leg!

7. **When you get flooded with positive memories, ask a close friend for a reality check.** Remind yourself that your attachment system is distorting your perspective on the relationship. Ask a friend to remind you how things *really* were. Even if you sometimes miss or idealize your ex, reality *will* slowly sink in.

8. **Deactivate: Write down all the reasons you wanted to**

leave. Your objective is to deactivate your attachment system. The best way to do so is to recall the bad moments in the relationship, and the best way to keep them fresh is to write them down. Take a peek at the list when those invasive positive memories creep into mind.

9. **Know that no matter how much pain you're going through now, it will pass.** Most people recover very well from a broken heart and eventually move on to greener pastures!

PART FOUR

The Secure Way—Sharpening
Your Relationship Skills

11.

Effective Communication: Getting the Message Across

USING EFFECTIVE COMMUNICATION TO CHOOSE THE RIGHT PARTNER

After a few dates with Ethan, Lauren found herself very confused. On their first date, they had gone to a romantic beach bar and spent several hours getting to know each other. At the end of the evening, he said a quick good-bye and disappeared. To her surprise he called again to ask her out, this time to a performance at a waterfront club. They both had a couple of drinks and spent hours dancing together. They even took a stroll along the beach, but again nothing happened, just an abrupt "we'll talk" when they parted. This pattern repeated itself one more time on their next date. Lauren, who has an anxious attachment style, thought that perhaps Ethan simply wasn't attracted to her. But then why was he still asking her out? Maybe he just wanted the companionship? She didn't want to stop seeing him without a bona fide reason, because she really liked him. A close friend encouraged her to stop speculating about the reasons for his behavior and simply ask.

Normally, Lauren wouldn't have had the courage—she would have been far too afraid of the hurtful response she might get. But she'd reached a point where she was no longer willing to waste precious time on the wrong person. So she did raise the subject with Ethan, tentatively at first, but she found herself speaking very directly as the conversation progressed: "I'm looking for more than something platonic. What is it that you have in mind?" Contrary to her assumption, she learned that he didn't find her unattractive. He said he really liked her and expressed his desire for finding a partner. But when she went a step further and asked specifically about his "no-touch" policy, he didn't have an answer and kept beating around the bush. Although she didn't come out of the conversation with a specific answer as to why he wasn't interested in physical contact, she did get a clear picture about their future together—there was none!

Lauren gave up thinking of him as a potential partner, but they remained friends. After Ethan confided in her about several other women he was dating who were obviously also becoming frustrated by his puzzling behavior, she finally put two and two together. The mystery around Ethan's conduct was not so mysterious after all—it became clear that he was having serious doubts about his sexual orientation. Lauren thanked God she'd had the guts to express her concerns early on, saving herself months of false hopes and certain rejection.

Lauren's story is an excellent example of the importance of effective communication. Expressing your needs and expectations to your partner in a direct, nonaccusatory manner is an incredibly powerful tool. Though it's used naturally by people with a secure attachment style, it is often counterintuitive for people whose attachment style is anxious or avoidant.

One straightforward conversation with Ethan put an end to all the guesswork and "theories" Lauren had built up in her mind. For Ethan it would have been convenient if Lauren had been willing to simply put up with his behavior indefinitely. He was getting what he wanted—a girlfriend to show off to friends and family (to get them off his back) and time to sort out his sexual orientation. But by expressing her needs, Lauren was able to look out for herself and avoid getting strung along by someone else's agenda. In this case, attachment style was not the underlying issue, but Lauren had no way of knowing this in advance. If Ethan's behavior was simply a manifestation of his attachment style, effective communication would have uncovered that as well, and they would have both benefited from discovering early on that their attachment styles were incompatible.

But what would have happened if Lauren had confronted him in this forthright way, causing him great embarrassment, only to discover that his behavior was the result of neither his attachment style nor his sexual orientation but of simple shyness? Well, we know someone who had just such an experience.

Tina's situation was very similar to Lauren's. On her third date with Serge, Tina was sitting on the sofa next to him watching a movie and wondering why he wasn't making a move. She'd also had her share of dead-end relationships and wasn't willing to waste too much time wondering what Serge's particular issue might be. So, affecting a coquettish smile, she simply said, "Can I have a kiss?" Though Serge was taken aback for a second and mumbled something under his breath, he collected himself and leaned over to kiss her. That was the last time his shyness was an issue in their relationship, which is still going strong three years later.

In this case, flirtatiously asking for a kiss was an eloquent use of effective communication. Tina expressed her needs, and although there was an awkward moment, her directness gave her relationship with Serge a tremendous push that brought them much closer, not only physically, but also emotionally. Even if Serge had reacted in some other way, and things had worked out differently, it would still have been helpful: People's response to effective communication is *always* very telling. It either allows you to avoid getting involved in a dead-end relationship, as in Lauren and Ethan's case, or it helps bring the relationship to a deeper level, as in Serge and Tina's case.

Effective communication works on the understanding that we all have very specific needs in relationships, many of which are determined by your attachment style. They aren't good or bad, they simply are what they are. If you're anxious, you have a strong need for closeness and have to be reassured at all times that your partner loves and respects you. If you're avoidant, you need to be able to maintain some distance, either emotional or physical, from your partner and preserve a large degree of separateness. In order to be happy in a relationship, we need to find a way to communicate our attachment needs clearly without resorting to attacks or defensiveness.

WHY USE EFFECTIVE COMMUNICATION?

Effective communication works to achieve two goals:

- **To choose the right partner.** Effective communication is the quickest, most direct way to determine whether your prospective partner will be able to meet your needs. Your date's response to effective communication can reveal more in five minutes than you could learn in months of dating without this kind of discourse. If the other person shows a sincere wish to understand your needs and put your well-being first, your future together has promise. If he or she brushes your concerns aside as insignificant, or makes you feel inadequate, foolish, or self-indulgent, you can conclude that this person doesn't sincerely have your best interests in mind and you are probably incompatible.

- **To make sure your needs are met in the relationship, whether it is a brand-new one or one of long standing.** By spelling out your needs, you are making it a lot easier for your partner to meet them. He or she doesn't need to guess whether something is bothering you—or what that something is.

The beauty of effective communication is that it allows you to turn a supposed weakness into an asset. If you need to be reassured a lot that your partner loves you and is attracted to you (at least in the initial phase of a relationship), instead of trying to conceal this wish because it is not socially acceptable to sound so needy, you state it as a given. When presented this way, you don't come off as either weak or needy but as self-confident and assertive. Of course, effective communication means that you communicate in a way that is inoffensive and does not put your partner on the spot, but allows them to be open with you without feeling attacked, criticized, or blamed.

Another advantage of effective communication is that it provides a role model for your partner. You set the tone for the relationship as one in which you can both be honest and in which each has the sacred responsibility to look out for the other's well-being. Once your partner sees that you can be so open, he or she will follow suit. As you saw in chapter 8, it's never too late to start using effective communication to improve your relationship. It's one of the most powerful tools secure people use in their everyday life, with their partner and kids, and at work. It can really transform the way you handle yourself with the people around you.

JUDGING THE RESPONSE

With effective communication, you might not be able to solve a problem or resolve your differences in one shot. But you can judge *immediately* how important your well-being is to your partner:

- Does s/he try to get to the bottom of your concerns?
- Does s/he respond to the issue at hand or does s/he try to dodge you?

- Does s/he take your concerns seriously or does s/he try to belittle you or make you feel foolish for raising them?
- Does s/he try to find ways to make you feel better or is s/he only busy acting defensive?
- Is s/he replying to your concerns only factually (as in a court of law) or is s/he also in tune with your emotional well-being?

If your partner is responsive and genuinely concerned about your happiness and security, you have a green light to go ahead with the relationship. If, however, your partner tries to evade important topics, acts defensively, or makes you feel foolish or needy, you should heed it as a serious warning sign.

WHY IT IS HARD FOR PEOPLE WITH AN INSECURE STYLE TO ADOPT EFFECTIVE COMMUNICATION

Effective communication almost seems like a no-brainer. After all, all people can do it once they set their mind to it, right? Well, yes, *as long as they are secure.* Often, insecure people cannot get in touch with what is really bothering them. They get overwhelmed by emotions and lash out. Studies show that people with a secure attachment style don't react so strongly, don't get overwhelmed as easily, and can thus calmly and effectively communicate their own feelings and tend to the needs of their partners. Secure people also believe that they are worthy of love and affection, and expect their partners to be responsive and caring. With these beliefs, it's easy to see why they don't let negative thoughts take over, how they can stay calm and collected and assume the other person will react positively. In fact, this attitude can be infectious. Nancy Collins of University of California–Santa Barbara, whose main research interests include the social and cognitive processes that shape close relationships in adulthood and the impact that these processes have on health and well-being, together with Stephen Read of the University of Southern California, who studies the neural network models of social reasoning and behavior, found that people with a secure attachment style seem to function as effective-communication coaches—they report being good at getting others to open up and talk about personal things. But what happens if you're not secure?

IF YOU'RE ANXIOUS . . .

When you start to feel something is bothering you in your relationship, you tend to quickly get flooded with negative emotions and think in extremes. Unlike your secure counterpart, you don't expect your partner to respond positively but anticipate the opposite. You perceive the relationship as something fragile and unstable that can collapse at any moment. These thoughts and assumptions make it hard for you to express your needs effectively. When you finally talk to your partner, you often do it in a way that is explosive, accusatory, critical, or threatening. Rather than giving you the reassurance you're seeking, your partner may withdraw. In fact, Collins and Read confirmed this in their study: Men who dated anxious partners reported self-disclosing less often and rated their general level of communication as lower than others. The result is that after expressing your needs in a way that pushes your partner away (instead of using effective communication), you then resort to protest behavior—expressing your need for closeness and reassurance by acting out. By doing so, you miss out on all the benefits of this powerful tool—unlike effective communication, protest behavior never gives you the opportunity to unequivocally address your concerns. Your partner may respond negatively, but you're never sure if he or she is responding to your need or to your protest behavior.

Say, for example, that you call your partner's cell phone incessantly because you fear he's cheating. He decides that he's had enough and breaks up with you. You're left second-guessing, wondering if you actually pushed him away by acting so clingy or if he decided that you really just weren't right for him. You don't get an answer to your original concern, which is whether he cares enough to listen to your worries, reassure you, and do whatever it takes to make you feel safe and loved.

Therefore, despite your understandable fear of getting hurt, we advise you to avoid protest behavior by taking a leap of faith and adopting effective communication. We can honestly say that everyone we've known who has used effective communication has been grateful for it in the long run. Often, effective communication brings about huge relief by showing you just how strongly your partner feels about you—and by strengthening the bond between you two. And even though in some instances the response may not be what you hoped for and you'll be convinced that you've ruined everything—if only you had said or done something else, he would surely have come around—we've never heard anyone say in retrospect that they regretted raising an important issue in a dating or relationship setting. In fact, they overwhelmingly express gratitude that effective communication got them that one step closer to their *long-term* goal of either finding the right person or strengthening their existing bond.

Take Hillary, for example. She was planning a romantic walk with Steve across the Brooklyn Bridge on a sunny Saturday morning, but when she called him he told her that he'd started doing his laundry and would call her later. Seeing that Hillary was upset, her friend convinced her to call him back and urge him to finish his laundry after the walk—it was such a beautiful spring day, after all. Reluctantly, Hillary made the call. Not only did Steve restate his decision to finish up the laundry, he decided he didn't want to get together at all that day! Hillary was devastated. She was furious with her friend for talking her into calling him. She felt that by showing too much interest, she'd ruined her chances with Steve. Months later, a mutual friend told her that Steve was deeply depressed following his bitter divorce and was far from being interested—or able—to start a new relationship. Hillary realized that pushing the issue that morning had saved her from the grief that Steve's emotional unavailability would have undoubtedly caused her. At the time, Hillary was very upset with her friend and blamed her for ruining her chances with Steve, but she later realized that her friend had taught her one of the most valuable lessons in relationships: how to effectively communicate her needs. This was the first time that Hillary felt certain that she fully and genuinely showed up in a relationship—no games played. Though things didn't work out with Steve, she knew that she did her best to make it happen. She also began to discover that more often than not, the reasons why people behave unkindly toward her have nothing to do with her attractiveness or desirability.

Here's another example of how just stating what you want, without any apologies, can be powerfully effective:

For years, Jena, afraid of sounding desperate, wasn't up front with the guys she dated about her great desire to get married and have children. When she turned 40 and her biological clock took precedence over everything else, she decided to tell potential partners on date number one that she not only wanted to be a mother, but was only interested in dating men who also wanted to have kids as soon as possible. Though she suspected—and rightly so—that most guys who heard this would run in the other direction, fear of rejection was no longer Jena's main concern. She did drive a few prospects away but ended up meeting Nate, who, far from being threatened, wanted the same thing. He found it refreshing that she knew what she wanted and wasn't afraid to say it. Using effective communication worked out well for her. Today she and Nate are the happy parents of two.

Like Jena and Hillary, you too can learn how to use effective communication, even though it can be a scary prospect if you have an anxious attachment style.

IF YOU ARE AVOIDANT . . .

Although there is nothing that brings two people closer than understanding and being understood by each other, effective communication has something to offer the avoidant person as well. As someone with an avoidant attachment style, you are often unaware of your need for distance and separateness—you feel the need to get away but don't understand why. When you get that feeling, you may assume that you're beginning to be less attracted to your partner, in which case, what is there to talk about? He or she is probably not "the one," so why prolong the agony? But then you find yourself in one failed relationship after another, repeating the same cycle again and again. If you are avoidant, the first step, therefore, is to acknowledge your need for space—whether emotional or physical—when things get too close, and then learn how to communicate that need. Explain to your partner in advance that you need some time alone when you feel things getting too mushy and that it's not a problem with him or her but rather your own need in *any* relationship (this bit is important!). This should quell their worries and somewhat calm their attachment system. They are then less likely to intensify their efforts to draw closer to you (which is what makes you uncomfortable the most). Thus, there is a better chance you'll avoid a full-blown pursuit-withdrawal dynamic with your partner.

Andres, who has an avoidant attachment style, had been married to Monica for about twenty-five years when he discovered that he had a slowly progressive autoimmune condition. It was incurable, he was told, but given his age, his life expectancy would probably not be severely impaired. It would require periodic lab tests, though. After the initial shock of the discovery, Andres was able to push the thoughts about his condition aside and move on with his life. Monica, however, wasn't able to do so. She believed that taking the "business-as-usual" approach was wrong. She tried to convince him on several occasions to get a second opinion and do a thorough search on the Internet about his condition. Andres would usually evade these conversations and brush her medical suggestions aside, but sometimes it led to severe clashes between them. Finally, after several months of frustration, he confronted Monica. He knows her involvement stems from worry and concern, but instead of helping, it only serves to remind him again and again of his condition. He trusted his doctor and felt that there was no need for further inquiry. He felt that Monica's behavior was not only ineffective in improving his health but also harmful to their relationship. Monica realized that she wasn't helping Andres—it was her way of dealing with such a diagnosis, but it wasn't his. She understood that she could be a better, more supportive partner by respecting his wishes instead of trying to force her own. Since then, Monica has been able to censor herself more (though not completely), which has allowed the clashes between them to diminish.

USING EFFECTIVE COMMUNICATION TO ENSURE YOUR NEEDS ARE MET IN THE RELATIONSHIP

Monique and Greg have been going out for a couple of months, and the Fourth of July is around the corner. Monique plans to celebrate the event with a group of friends, but she hasn't invited Greg to join her, at least not yet. Greg is becoming more and more upset by this. He's worried about what this means. Does Monique only see him as someone temporary in her life? Perhaps she's embarrassed by him and doesn't want to introduce him to her friends? Greg doesn't want to confront her directly for fear it will make him seem too eager and needy. Instead he decides to throw out hints: "I'm not sure yet what I should do on the Fourth. I've had a few offers, but I can't decide if any of them are worthwhile." In

Attached

fact, he doesn't have other plans, but he doesn't want to sound like he's fishing for an invitation. Monique doesn't pick up on his cues; she assumes he really is sizing up his options and tries to help out. At this point Greg decides to just give up, thinking that if, after all these hints, Monique still chooses not to invite him, she obviously doesn't want him to come. Anger builds up inside him and he decides he will have to think long and hard about whether Monique is really the girl for him.

But what if Greg used effective communication? He has an anxious attachment style, and the kind of dialogue required by effective communication does not come naturally to him. He is more accustomed to turning to protest behavior. He decides, however, to take a different approach. He turns to Monique: "I'd like to spend the Fourth of July together. Would you like to come with me and my friends or would you prefer that I join you?" Monique responds that she hadn't thought of inviting him because spending an evening with her old crowd from high school didn't sound like the kind of thing he'd enjoy, but if he was game, why not? A simple question got Greg the answer that he wanted. Even more significantly, after that first successful precedent, they both find it easier to talk openly to each other.

What if Monique responded differently and Greg's request had been rebuffed? As always with effective communication, you win either way. Even if Monique had ignored his request and quickly changed the subject, he would have learned something very telling. A red flag based on reality—and not on Greg's anxious assumptions—would have been raised about Monique's ability to respond to his needs and sensitivities. We're not suggesting that Greg should leave Monique immediately if she reacted in this way, but it would expose a smoking gun. Two or three such evading tactics would probably inspire Greg to look for love elsewhere.

WHEN SHOULD I USE EFFECTIVE COMMUNICATION?

When asked when to use effective communication, our automatic response is "always!" But then we often hear, "Do I have to bring up every single relationship issue right away? I'm anxious—that would mean expressing every worry and doubt that crosses my mind—and God knows there are plenty of them." Usually, if you address things that are bothering you from the get-go and receive a positive response, your whole demeanor will change. Worries and fears surface more when you are not communicating your concerns and are letting things build up.

But at least until you feel completely comfortable using effective communication, we suggest following this basic rule of thumb:

- **If you are anxious**—turn to effective communication when you feel you are starting to resort to protest behavior. When something your partner has said or done (or refrained from saying or doing) has activated your attachment system to the point where you feel you're on the verge of acting out—by not answering his or her calls, threatening to leave, or engaging in any other form of protest behavior—stop yourself. Then figure out what your real needs are and use effective communication instead.

But only after you've thoroughly calmed down (which for someone anxious can sometimes take a day or two).

- **If you are avoidant**—the surefire sign that you need to use effective communication is when you feel an irrepressible need to bolt. Use effective communication to explain to your partner that you need some space and that you'd like to find a way of doing so that is acceptable to him or her. Suggest a few alternatives, making sure that the other person's needs are taken care of. By doing so, you're more likely to get the breathing space you need.

IT'S NEVER TOO LATE TO USE EFFECTIVE COMMUNICATION, EVEN IF YOU START OFF ON THE WRONG FOOT

Larry got a disturbing e-mail from work one Saturday while Sheila, his partner of seven years, was out seeing a friend. When she came home to pick up her things for the gym, Larry became anxious and upset: "You're going out again? You just got home! I never get to see you on weekends!" Even as he was saying this, Larry knew that he wasn't being fair. Sheila was taken aback by the unwarranted attack—he'd known of her plans, and before confirming them, she had even offered to stay home with him if he had wanted her to. The atmosphere became tense and neither said a word for some time. After reading something to calm down, Larry realized what his behavior was really all about: He was edgy because of the e-mail from work and wanted the security of having Sheila close by, but wasn't comfortable asking her to change her plans. He'd instinctively launched into protest behavior, picking a fight just to engage her. He apologized to Sheila for not expressing his needs effectively and explained the situation. Once the true message got through, she calmed down as well. She gave him the support that he needed and he insisted that she go to the gym.

Although Larry initially resorted to protest behavior, he discovered that, with a receptive partner, effective communication, even when employed late in the game, can diffuse a stressful situation.

THE FIVE PRINCIPLES OF EFFECTIVE COMMUNICATION

Like the concept of effective communication, the principles are also very straightforward:

1. **Wear your heart on your sleeve.** Effective communication requires being genuine and completely honest about your feelings. Be emotionally brave!

2. **Focus on your needs.** The idea is to get your needs across. When expressing your needs, we are always referring to needs that take your partner's well-being into consideration as well. If they end up hurting him or her, you're sure to get hurt too; after all, you and your partner are an emotional unit. When expressing your needs, it's helpful to use verbs such as *need, feel,* and *want,* which focus on what you are trying to accomplish and not on your partner's shortcomings:

- *"I need to feel confident in the relationship. When you chat up the waitress, I feel like I'm on thin ice."*
- *"I feel devalued when you contradict me in front of your friends. I need to feel that you respect my opinions."*
- *"I want to know I can trust you. When you go to bars with your friends, I worry a lot that you'll cheat on me."*

3. **Be specific.** If you speak in general terms, your partner may not understand exactly what you really need, which may lower his or her chances of getting it right. State precisely what is bothering you:

- *When you don't stay the night . . .*
- *When you don't check up on me every day . . .*
- *When you said you loved me and then took it back . . .*

4. **Don't blame.** Never make your partner feel selfish, incompetent, or inadequate. Effective communication is not about highlighting the other person's shortcomings, and making accusations will quickly lead you away from the point and into a dueling match. Make sure to find a time when you're calm to discuss things. You'll find that attempting to use effective communication when you're on the verge of exploding is a contradiction in terms— you'll most likely sound angry or judgmental.

5. **Be assertive and nonapologetic.** Your relationship needs are valid—period. Though people with different attachment styles may not see your concerns as legitimate, they're essential for *your* happiness, and expressing them

authentically is crucial to effective communication. This point is especially important if you have an anxious attachment style, because our culture encourages you to believe that many of your needs are illegitimate. But whether they are legitimate or not for someone else is beside the point. They are essential for your happiness, and that is what's important.

A New Miranda's Law of Dating: Effective Communication Right from the Start

In 1966, Miranda warnings were mandated by the Supreme Court. Police were required to Mirandize those under arrest by reading them their rights: *You have the right to remain silent. Anything you say can and will be used against you in a court of law. You have the right to an attorney present during questioning. If you cannot afford an attorney, one will be appointed for you. Do you understand these rights?*

A colleague of ours, Diane, used to joke about guys who would "Mirandize" her, i.e., inform her of what she had a "right" to expect when dating them. "I don't think that I'm ready for commitment," they would say, meaning, "If it doesn't work out, don't say I didn't warn you." Apparently, like the police, who are protected legally while they interrogate a suspect, these guys felt absolved of any emotional responsibility toward Diane once they had laid down "the law."

Using attachment principles, you can create your own secure (rather than avoidant) Miranda rights outlining your belief that when people fall in love, they are all but putting their soul in their partner's hand for safekeeping, and that you both have the responsibility to keep it safe and make it prosper.

By conveying to your partner a secure working model of love and relationships, you are setting yourself up for a secure connection from the get-go:

- You are wearing your heart on your sleeve.
- You are able to gauge the other person's response.
- You are allowing both yourself and your partner to strive for a secure, mutually dependent bond.

COMMUNICATING EFFECTIVELY IOI

Getting Started

When you are not use to effective communication, it can be extremely helpful to formulate a script of the message you want to convey. It's best not to attempt this when you are upset, and it's also important to ignore the advice of friends who suggest indirect methods of trying to get your needs met, such as making your partner jealous. If possible, ask your attachment-designated person—ADP (see chapter 9)—or friend who has a secure attachment style or who is familiar with the principles of effective communication to help you compose the right words. When you are sure of the content, recite it to yourself until you feel comfortable with the way it sounds. Having everything written down can help you get over fears about getting cold feet or forgetting your "lines," and make it easier for you to address your partner with confidence. Once you get the hang of it and experience the positive effect it has on your life, using effective communication will become second nature.

Exercise: Answer the Following Questions to Determine the Topic of Your Script

Why do I feel uneasy or insecure (activated or deactivated) in this relationship? What specific actions by my partner make me feel this way? (The relationship inventory in chapter 9 can help you with the process.)

1. _____
2. _____
3. _____

What specific action/s by my partner would make me feel more secure and loved?

1. _____
2. _____
3. _____

Which of the above actions do I feel most comfortable bringing up and discussing?

_____

_____

Use your response to this last question to guide you toward the topic of your first effective communication. Now create a short script that focuses on that issue, while adhering to the five principles of effective communication.

My Script:

_____

_____

_____

_____

_____

Review the examples that follow. Notice how ineffective communication can be interpreted in different ways while effective communication has only one specific meaning. That's why your partner's response to effective communication is much more telling than his or her response to ineffective communication or protest behavior.

Effective Communication

Situation	Ineffective communication (Protest behavior)	Effective communication
He's very busy at work and you hardly get to see him.	Call him every couple of hours to make sure you're on his mind.	Tell him you miss him and are having a hard time adjusting to his new work schedule, even though you understand that it's temporary.
She doesn't really listen to you when you're talking, which makes you feel unimportant and misunderstood.	Get up in the middle of the conversation and go to another room (hoping she'll follow you and apologize).	Make it clear that it's not enough that she listens without responding. Emphasize that you value her opinion above anyone's and it's important to you to know what she thinks.
He talks about his ex-girlfriend, which makes you feel insecure.	Tell him it's pathetic that he's still talking about his ex. *or* Bring up other guys you went out with to let him know how bad it feels.	Let him know that conversations about his ex-girlfriend make you feel inadequate and unsure of where you stand, that you need to feel secure in order to be happy with someone.
He always calls at the last minute to make plans.	Tell him you're busy whenever he does that so that eventually he'll learn to call well in advance.	Explain that you feel unsettled not knowing when and if you'll see him and that it's better for you to at least have a ballpark schedule of when you'll get together ahead of time.

Situation	Ineffective communication (Protest behavior)	Effective communication
She screens your calls a lot and gets back to you in her own good time.	Grin and bear it.	Convey how important it is to you to return *her* calls promptly and how good it would feel if she was to do the same.
He hasn't called for a few days. You're worried that he wants to end the relationship.	When he finally calls, tell him you're busy. That'll show him.	Inform him that it is hurtful when he disappears and that one of the things that you need most in a relationship is for your boyfriend to make you a priority whenever possible.

It's important to remember that even with effective communication, some problems won't be solved immediately. What's vital is your partner's response—whether he or she is concerned about your well-being, has your best interests in mind, and is willing to work on things.

12.

Working Things Out: Five Secure Principles for Dealing with Conflict

CAN FIGHTING MAKE US *HAPPIER*?

A major misconception about conflict in romantic relationships is that people in good relationships should fight very little. There's an expectation that, if well matched, you and your partner will see eye to eye on most matters and argue rarely, if at all. Sometimes arguments are even considered to be "proof" that two people are incompatible or that a relationship is derailing. Attachment theory shows us that these assumptions are unsubstantiated; all couples—even secure ones—have their fair share of fights. What does differentiate between couples and affect their satisfaction levels in their relationships is not how much they disagree, but how they disagree and what they disagree about. Attachment researchers have learned that conflicts can serve as an opportunity for couples to get closer and deepen their bond.

There are two main kinds of conflict—the bread-and-butter

type and the intimacy-centered type. In chapter 8, we witnessed what happens when people with diametrically opposed intimacy needs get together and, despite their best intentions, struggle to find common ground. We saw how these conflicting needs can spill over into every area of life and often result in one party making all the concessions. Bread-and-butter conflicts are typically devoid of intimacy struggles.

BREAD-AND-BUTTER CONFLICTS

As the name suggests, bread-and-butter conflicts are those disputes that inevitably arise when separate wills and personalities share daily life—which channel to watch, what temperature to set the air conditioning on, whether to order Chinese or Indian. Such disagreements are actually good because they force you to live in relation to someone else and learn to compromise. One of the cruelest punishments a human being can endure is solitary confinement; we're social creatures and live best in relation to others. Although at times being flexible in our thinking and actions means stepping outside of our comfort zone, it keeps our minds young and active, even allowing brain cells to regenerate.

But what looks good on paper—taking another's needs and preferences into account, even when they oppose our own—isn't always easy to carry out. Interestingly, people with a secure attachment style instinctively know how to do this. They're able to lower the heat during an argument and take the edge off an escalating conflict. If you've ever found yourself caught off guard during a disagreement by the other person's genuine interest in your concerns and willingness to consider them, you were probably disagreeing with someone secure. But is a natural inclination helpful for those of us who haven't been bestowed with these skills?

Actually, when we take a closer look, we can see that there's a method behind the secures' instinctive behavior. It's less about their magical powers than about their helpful practices. Not only have we identified five specific actions that people with a secure attachment style use to diffuse and resolve conflict, but we believe that they can be learned. Adult attachment theory has proven time and again that when it comes to attachment style, we're malleable. And it's never too late to learn new relationship skills.

THE SECURE PRINCIPLES FOR MAKING CONFLICT WORK

Let's take a closer look at the five principles that secure people use when they're having a disagreement with their partner.

Five Secure Principles for Resolving Conflict
•
1. Show basic concern for the other person's well-being.
2. Maintain focus on the problem at hand.
3. Refrain from generalizing the conflict.
4. Be willing to engage.
5. Effectively communicate feelings and needs.

1. Show basic concern for the other person's well-being: A cottage in the Berkshires

Frank loves the outdoors and the summer home in the Berkshires that he inherited from his parents. Sandy hates it. She dreads the hassle of packing and unpacking and the traffic they always get stuck in on the long drives. To her, the whole experience is more trouble than it's worth. It took a few bitter fights before they realized that each partner insisting on his or her wishes and ignoring the other's ended up making both of them unhappy. They found a system that worked despite their inherent differences in the way they wish to spend their downtime. Today, when Sandy senses that city life is becoming too much for Frank, she takes one for the team and they venture to the woods. Similarly, when Frank sees that Sandy is feeling overwhelmed by traveling, they stay in the city—sometimes for long stretches of time. On those occasions he makes sure to schedule outdoor activities in order to keep his sanity. It's not a perfect system, and sometimes one of them gets upset and complains, but they're able to work it out, each accommodating the other as best they can.

Frank and Sandy both understand the fundamental premise of a good relationship—that the other person's well-being is as important as your own. Ignoring your partner's needs will have a direct impact on your own emotions, satisfaction level, and even physical health. We often view conflict as a zero-sum game: either you get your way or I get mine. But attachment theory shows us that our happiness is actually dependent on our mate's and vice versa. The two are inextricable. Despite their divergent wishes, Frank and Sandy engage in a kind of back and forth synchronicity that gives them both the satisfaction of knowing that the other person is attuned to their needs. From an attachment perspective, this is a hugely rewarding experience.

2. Maintain focus on the problem at hand:
George's messy place

"On one of our first dates," Kelly recalls, "George and I stopped by his apartment, but he didn't invite me up. He said it was being renovated and he felt uncomfortable having me see it that way. Being a suspicious person, his excuse didn't make sense to me. I leapt to conclusions, conjuring up images of an extra toothbrush in his bathroom and another woman's underwear on his bed. He noticed my mood change and asked me what was going on. I told him that it was obvious he had something to hide, and our date ended on a sour note.

"The next evening, however, George invited me over. He buzzed me in, and as I was going up the stairs, he opened his door and with a sweep of his arm gestured me in, saying 'Welcome, welcome, welcome!' The place was indeed a mess, but we both laughed about it and all the bad feelings were gone."

George was able to turn the situation around because he has a secure attachment style. Although his responses might seem natural, if we look a bit more closely, we can see that they wouldn't come so naturally to everybody. George remained very focused on the issue at hand. While Kelly, who has an anxious attachment style, veered off the topic, making personal accusations, George was able to see through her protest behavior and home in on what was really bothering her. His behavior fits well with research findings. Garry Creasey, the head of the attachment lab at Illinois State University, who has a particular interest in conflict management from an attachment perspective, together with Matthew Hesson-McInnis, also from the department of psychology at Illinois State University, found that secures are better able to understand their partner's perspective and maintain focus on the problem. By responding to Kelly's fears, and addressing them quickly and effectively, George prevented further conflict. His ability to build a secure connection benefits them both: Kelly learns that she has a partner who feels responsible for her well-being, and George discovers that he is accepted as he is, clutter and all. When there's a willingness to resolve a specific problem, people feel that they're being heard and it brings both parties closer together.

But secure people aren't always able to resolve arguments in such an elegant manner. They too can lose their temper and overlook their partner's needs.

3. Refrain from generalizing the conflict:
The shopping trip

Though both Terry and Alex, who are in their mid-fifties, have a secure attachment style, they've engaged in an ongoing fighting ritual for more than thirty years. Terry will send Alex to the supermarket with a very detailed shopping list—crushed tomatoes, whole wheat bread, and a package of Barilla pasta. A couple of hours later Alex will come back with similar, but not the exact, products. He'll have purchased a different brand of pasta and tomato paste instead of crushed tomatoes. Terry gets upset, declares the items unusable, and dramatically proclaims that she'll have to go to the store herself. Alex responds by losing his temper, grabs the groceries, and storms out of the house. He returns with the correct items, but the day has been ruined by their confrontation.

Even though Terry and Alex care deeply about each other,

they've never really taken a good look at their fighting ritual. If they had, they would have realized the value in finding a different solution. Alex is a space cadet; he just doesn't seem to be able to pay attention to details, so why put both of them through a challenge he can't meet? For Terry these small details are crucial—she couldn't overlook them even if she tried. This doesn't mean Terry should have to take the entire burden on herself, however. A creative solution is in order. Terry can call Alex at the supermarket to make sure he's putting the correct items in the basket, she can place the order online and have him pick it up, or she can go herself while he helps with chores at home. They have to find a path of less resistance and go with it.

One thing is notable, though. Despite their fussing, they do manage to steer clear of a number of destructive pitfalls. Most important, they don't let the conflict spill over into other areas or get out of control. They avoid making disparaging comments or hurtful generalizations about each other. They keep the argument restricted to the topic at hand and don't blow things out of proportion. Even though Terry angrily threatens to go to the store herself—and on occasion does—she doesn't expand it to "I've had it with you" or "You know what? You can cook your own dinner, I'm leaving!"

4. Be willing to engage

In all three conflicts above, whether resolved peacefully or explosively, the secure partner (or partners) remains "present" both physically and emotionally. George is instinctively able to contain Kelly's personal attack and, taking responsibility for her hurt feelings, turns the situation around while remaining engaged. Had he been avoidant or even anxious, he might have responded to Kelly's silent treatment by withdrawing and creating even more distance and hostility.

Frank and Sandy could also each have decided to dig in their heels. Sandy could have said, "You know what? Do whatever you want, but I'm spending my weekends in the city!" and refused to discuss things further. Frank could have done the same. Locked in a stalemate, they'd have spent many unhappy weekends missing each other. Only because they're both willing to stay and deal with the issue do they find a resolution that they can both live with and in the process learn to be more in tune to each other's needs.

5. Effectively communicate feelings and needs: Visiting the sister-in-law

Because Tom's job is so hectic, Rebecca barely gets to see him during the week, and she often feels very alone. On Saturdays, she usually visits her sister, who lives close by. Tom doesn't typically join her for these visits; he likes to stay home and veg out on the couch. Generally, this is fine with her, but this Saturday, after a particularly long week at work, when Tom was even more absent than usual, she becomes very insistent that he come along. Tom, exhausted from his work week, is adamant about not wanting to go. Rebecca won't take no for an answer and pushes the issue. He reacts by clamming up even more. Finally she tells him he's being selfish, he ends up in front of the TV not talking, and she ends up going alone.

Rebecca acts in a way that is very typical of people with an anxious attachment style. Because her husband's being at work more than usual during the week has activated her attachment system, she feels a need to reconnect. What she needs most is to feel that Tom is available to her—that he cares and wants to be with her. However, instead of *saying* this directly and explaining what is bothering her, she uses protest behavior—accusing him of being selfish and insisting that he come to her sister's. Tom is bewildered that Rebecca is suddenly behaving so irrationally—after all, they have an understanding that he doesn't have to go to her sister's.

How different Tom's reaction might be if Rebecca simply said, "I know you hate going to my sister's, but it would mean the world to me if you could come this one time. I've hardly seen you all week and I don't want to miss out on any more time together."

Effectively expressing your emotional needs is even better than the other person magically reading your mind. It means that you're an active agent who can be heard, and it opens the door for a much richer emotional dialogue. Even if Tom still chose not to join Rebecca, if he understood how she felt, he could find another way to reassure her: "If you really want me to go, I will. But I also want to relax. How about we go out tonight—just the two of us? Would that make you feel better? You don't really want me at your sister's anyway, do you? I will get in the way of the two of you catching up."

Preventing Conflict—Attachment Biology 101

When it comes to conflict, it's not always about who did what to whom, or how to compromise, or even how to express yourself more effectively. Sometimes, understanding the basic biology of attachment helps you prevent conflict before it even happens. Oxytocin, a hormone and neuropeptide that has gotten a lot of press coverage in recent years, plays a major role in attachment processes and serves several purposes: It causes women to go into labor, strengthens attachment, and serves as a social cohesion hormone by increasing trust and cooperation. We get a boost of oxytocin in our brain during orgasm and even when we cuddle—which is why it's been tagged the "cuddle hormone."

How is oxytocin related to conflict reduction? Sometimes we spend less quality time with our partner—especially when other demands on us are pressing. However, neuroscience findings suggest that we should change our priorities. By forgoing closeness with our partners, we are also missing our oxytocin boost—making us less agreeable to the world around us and more vulnerable to conflict.

The next time you decide to skip the Sunday morning cuddle in bed for a chance to catch up on your work—think again. This small act might be enough to immunize your relationship against conflict for the next few days.

WHY INSECURE PEOPLE DON'T APPROACH CONFLICT HEAD-ON

Several aspects of the anxious and avoidant mind-sets make it difficult for them to adopt secure conflict resolution principles.

For the anxious, conflict can trigger very basic concerns about their partner's responsiveness to their needs and about rejection or abandonment. When a dispute arises, they experience many negative thoughts and react by using protest behavior, aimed at getting their partner's attention. They may make strong accusations, cry, or give their partner the silent treatment. Fearful that their partner is likely to be inattentive to their needs, they feel they need to really leave their mark in order to be heard. Their response, though often dramatic, is usually ineffective.

People with an avoidant attachment style are also threatened by the possibility that their mate won't really be there for them when needed. However, to deal with these beliefs, they adopt the opposite approach—they suppress their need for intimacy by shutting down emotionally and adopting a defensive air of independence. The more personal the conflict becomes, the stronger their urge grows to distance themselves from the situation. To do this they use deactivating strategies—such as finding fault with their partner—in order to feel less close to him or her.

Another study by Gary Creasey, together with two graduate students at the time, Kathy Kershaw and Ada Boston, found that both anxious people and avoidant people use fewer positive conflict-resolution tactics, express more aggression, and tend more toward withdrawal and escalation of conflict than secure people. Perhaps the similarities in their attitude toward conflict—that is, their basic belief in their partner's unavailability and their difficulty expressing their needs effectively—explain this finding.

PAUL AND JACKIE'S KID-SIZED PROBLEM

Though Jackie and Paul have been seeing each other for over a year and spend most nights together, Paul has three children that Jackie has never met. Her friends and family are worried about this situation and wonder where the relationship going.

Jackie has tried to address the matter, but Paul feels the time is still not right—maintaining stability in his children's life is of the utmost importance to him. Every other weekend, when Paul has the kids, he is off-limits to Jackie, who feels that if she raises the subject again, she might tip the relationship over the edge. Even on appropriate occasions—when Paul told her how much he loved her and talked about buying a house together—Jackie remained quiet about the kids and didn't reciprocate his declarations of love. She feels that if Paul really wanted them to be close, he would let her into his life completely, kids and all.

When Jackie's parents visit for dinner, Paul keeps talking about his kids and how wonderful they are. After dessert, Jackie's father invites Paul for a short walk. He tells him that his kids sound wonderful and he's hoping that Jackie will get to meet them soon, because he and his wife really like Paul and want to see the relationship grow. Paul assures him that he's very serious about the relationship. Neither of them tells Jackie about their talk.

The following week, Jackie has no idea why Paul is so quiet and answers her questions with only "Yes," "No," or "I don't know." Finally, she asks him what's wrong. He responds by lashing out, complaining that her father criticized him for talking about his kids, and reminds her of the many times he has expressed his feelings, only to have her not reciprocate. She replies that it's hard to open up when he's shutting her out of such a big part of his life. Rather than engaging in the discussion, he gets up, packs his belongings, and leaves, saying that he needs "some space." He returns several weeks later, but they still avoid discussing the matter and revert to the status quo.

Typical of people who have an insecure attachment style, both Jackie and Paul break almost every secure rule for handling conflict. Neither effectively communicates their needs and both avoid directly addressing the issue at hand—introducing Jackie to Paul's kids—but each for a different reason. Paul has a very firm opinion on the matter—he doesn't want his kids to meet someone unless it's very serious—and Jackie never reciprocated his love declarations. It doesn't occur to him to ask Jackie if it bothers her that they are separated every other weekend. Though he says he loves her, this doesn't translate into thinking that her feelings should be considered when it comes to his children (a characteristically avoidant attitude). He also assumes that if she doesn't often raise the topic of wanting to meet his children, she can't care that much.

Jackie, on the other hand, doesn't talk anymore about meeting his kids because she's anxious and worries that by making demands she may put the relationship in jeopardy. She fears that Paul may decide she's "just not worth the effort."

Paul also avoids secure principles when he chooses not to tell Jackie about his conversation with her father. Worse still, when they finally do talk about the issue, instead of engaging in the topic, Paul withdraws completely. Paul bottles up his anger for so long that by the time Jackie asks him what's wrong, he's at the end of his rope and is only able to attack her. Jackie, who is also insecure, isn't able to save the situation; instead of trying to soothe him and calm things down, she resorts to counterattacks. Being anxious, she interprets Paul's words as a personal rejection and responds defensively. Unfortunately, neither can see beyond their own hurt to comprehend the larger picture or what is going on with the other person.

As a rule of thumb, sensitive topics—like meeting a partner's children—should always be on the table. Assume that they're important, even if they aren't raised. You might not necessarily reach an immediate resolution, but at least you'll be open to hearing each other, and neither of you will be burying hurt feelings that will burst out uncontrollably sometime in the future. And of course, there is a better chance the issue will be resolved if it is discussed rather than ignored.

HOW TO MAKE SECURE PRINCIPLES WORK FOR YOU

Insecure assumptions interfere with conflict resolution. Specifically, being centered on your own needs and hurts can cause a lot of trouble. Fear that someone isn't as emotionally involved as you, or doesn't want to be as close as you'd like to be, is understandable. But in conflict situations, such preoccupations can be very damaging. Try to keep a number of truths in mind when you are in the midst of a fight:

- A single fight is not a relationship breaker.
- Express your fears! Don't let them dictate your actions. If you're afraid that s/he wants to reject you, say so.
- Don't assume you are to blame for your partner's bad mood. It is most likely *not* because of you.
- Trust that your partner *will* be caring and responsive and go ahead and express your needs.
- Don't expect your partner to know what you're thinking. If you haven't told him/her what's on your mind, s/he doesn't know!

- Don't assume that you understand what your partner means. When in doubt, ask.

A general word of advice: It's always more effective to assume the *best* in conflict situations. In fact, expecting the worst—which is typical of people with insecure attachment styles—often acts as a self-fulfilling prophecy. If you assume your partner will act hurtfully or reject you, you automatically respond defensively—thus starting a vicious cycle of negativity. Though you may have to talk yourself into believing the "positive truths" above (even if only halfheartedly at first), it is well worth the effort. In most cases, they will steer the dialogue in the right direction.

In sum, these are the habits you should keep away from during fights:

Insecure Conflict Strategies to Avoid

1. Getting sidetracked from the real problem.
2. Neglecting to effectively communicate your feelings and needs.
3. Reverting to personal attacks and destructiveness.
4. Reacting "tit for tat" to a partner's negativity with more negativity.
5. Withdrawing.
6. Forgetting to focus on the other's well-being.

Paul and Jackie's conflict is really intimacy-centered and not of the bread-and-butter type. We brought it up to demonstrate how easy it is to hit almost all of the "don'ts" listed above in a single dispute. Despite their love for each other, they (1) get easily sidetracked from the real problem ("Your father criticized me for talking about my children . . ."); they (2) obviously never effectively communicate their needs and feelings. A lot is left unsaid, especially by Jackie, who (5) uses emotional withdrawal and doesn't respond to Paul's attempts to get close in other ways. When they finally do talk, after a week of silence (5 again), they (4) engage in a tit for tat. Both are certainly also engrossed in their own concerns and (6) have great difficulty focusing on the other's well-being throughout their relationship and particularly when arguing.

A WORKSHOP
IN CONFLICT STRATEGIES

The first step toward identifying your own conflict tactics and changing them is to learn to recognize effective and ineffective conflict strategies. Take a look at the following situations and try to determine whether the couples deal with their differences using secure or insecure principles. If you think the principles used are insecure, list the secure principles that could be used instead.

1. Marcus booked a (mostly) singles cruise to Brazil before he and Daria started dating six months ago. Daria doesn't feel comfortable with Marcus going on such a

trip without her, and she doesn't like cruises. When she raises the subject to Marcus, he responds, "So I have to do everything with you now? You don't like stuff like that anyway, so why do you care? Besides, I've already paid for it. What do you want me to do, lose $3,000?"

Marcus's reaction is:
☐ Secure
☐ Insecure

Insecure tactics Marcus used:

_____

_____

Secure tactics Marcus could use:

_____

_____

Answer: Insecure. Marcus uses a whole slew of insecure tactics. He generalizes the conflict by attacking her ("What do you want me to do, lose $3,000?") and making her sound needy and overly reliant ("So I have to do everything with you now?"). He doesn't maintain focus on the problem, which is Daria's concern about the possibility that he won't remain faithful. He prefers to veer off the topic and make it about money and Daria's neediness.

Secure tactics Marcus could use: The best piece of advice for Marcus would be to maintain focus on the problem at hand. Daria's concern is real, and as long as he doesn't address it, this issue will never really be resolved.

2. Following her boyfriend's response in situation 1, Daria caves in. She apologizes for bringing up the issue. After all, this is a trip he'd planned before they even met. She feels bad that she's being so unreasonable, demanding, and dependent.

Daria's reaction is:
☐ Secure
☐ Insecure

Insecure tactics Daria used:

_____

_____

Secure tactics Daria could use:

_____

_____

Answer: Insecure. What's the matter with Daria? He's going on a singles cruise to Brazil six months into their relationship? She should by all means express her dismay. But instead of openly talking about her concerns, she backs down. She fears that because she spoke her mind, the relationship may end, so she tries to undo the damage by apologizing for raising the subject in the first place. By doing so Daria is agreeing to a new unspoken pact in the relationship: that her feelings and concerns are not that important.

Secure tactics Daria could use: She should effectively communicate her needs; tell Marcus about her concerns, and how anxious the upcoming vacation makes her feel about the future of their relationship. Marcus's reaction to her use of effective communication will be very significant. If he continues to belittle her and devalue her feelings, then she must ask herself whether she wants to be with someone like that for the long-term.

3. On a car ride, Ruth is telling John how concerned she is about their daughter's difficulties in math. John nods throughout the conversation but doesn't say much. After a few minutes, Ruth lashes out: "Why is this only my problem? She's your daughter too, but you don't seem to care. Aren't you worried about her?" John is taken aback by the attack. After a minute or so, he says, "I'm really exhausted and the driving is sapping all of my energy. I am very worried about this too, but I can barely concentrate on the road as it is."

John's reaction is:
□ Secure
□ Insecure

Insecure tactics John used:

_____

_____

Secure tactics John could use:

_____

_____

Answer: Secure. Secure people aren't saints! They can get tired and feel impatient at times, and their minds drift like everyone else's. The key is how they react once conflict arises. Notice how John doesn't retaliate or act defensive when Ruth attacks him. He maintains focus on the problem, answers in a straightforward way ("I'm really exhausted . . ."), and shows a genuine awareness for his wife's well-being by validating her concern ("I am very worried about this too").

Secure tactics John could use: John did a pretty good job; he averted an unnecessary escalation and calmed his partner down. Imagine if he'd snapped, "Goddamnit! Can't you see how tired I am? What do you want to do, get us in an accident?" Fortunately, he understood that his wife's accusation came from a place of distress rather than criticism, and he tackled the real problem, assuring her that they're partners where their daughter's welfare is concerned.

4. Steve, who has been dating Mia for a few weeks, calls her on Friday afternoon to ask if she'd like to join him and his friends that night at the local bar. Mia gets upset because Steve almost always wants to meet her with his friends, while she prefers a one-on-one rendezvous. "You're really scared of being alone with me, huh? I don't bite, you know," she says half jokingly. After an awkward silence, Steve replies, "Well, call me later if you want to go," and hangs up.

   Steve's reaction is:
   ☐ Secure
   ☐ Insecure

Insecure tactics Steve used:

_____

_____

Secure tactics Steve could use:

_____

_____

    Mia's reaction is:
    ☐ Secure
    ☐ Insecure

Insecure tactics Mia used:

_____

_____

Secure tactics Mia could use:

_____

_____

Answer: Steve—Insecure. Steve tries to avert a confrontation or an intimate conversation and withdraws instead of engaging. He doesn't try to find out what was on Mia's mind; he simply vanishes.

Secure tactics he could use: For starters, it seems that Steve is not really interested in anything serious. Otherwise he probably wouldn't choose to bring an entourage on every date. If, however, he does want to make the relationship work, Steve should stay focused on the problem and ask Mia what she meant by her statement. Granted, she did sound a bit cynical, but if Steve were smart (and secure), he wouldn't take it personally. He would try to see what was on her mind and how it could be used to take the relationship to a higher (and more intimate) level.

Answer: Mia—Insecure. But what about Mia? Her reaction was also insecure. Her attempt to effectively communicate her needs sounded a bit too much like an attack. She will now be left wondering, did I upset him? Did he think I was criticizing him?

Secure tactics Mia could use: Mia could have said something like, "You know, I'd rather not be with the crowd all the time. I enjoy being alone with you; how about we make plans for us?" (effectively communicating her needs). Steve's reaction would have revealed whether he's able to listen to what his partner wants and accommodate her needs.

5. While sitting at a sidewalk café, Emma notices her boyfriend Todd checking out other women as they walk by. "I really hate it when you do that. It's so humiliating," she says.

   "What do you mean?" he responds innocently.

   "You know exactly what I mean. You're staring."

   "That's ridiculous! Where do you want me to look? And even if I was looking, show me one guy who doesn't check out pretty women. It means absolutely nothing."

   Todd's reaction is:
   ☐ Secure
   ☐ Insecure

Insecure tactics Todd used:

_____

_____

Secure tactics Todd could use:

_____

_____

    Emma's reaction is:
    □ Secure
    □ Insecure

Insecure tactics Emma used:

_____

_____

Secure tactics Emma could use:

_____

_____

Answer: Todd—Insecure. Todd evades Emma's underlying concern—feeling unattractive and unappreciated when he checks out other women. Instead, he reverts to withdrawal, as opposed to engagement. At first he has "no idea" what she's talking about, and later he minimizes the importance of her argument by saying that it's just a natural part of being male. This is ineffective communication at its worst. Nothing gets resolved. She'll continue to feel upset by his behavior and he'll feel justified and self-righteous about continuing it.

Secure tactics Todd could use: The secure approach would have been to show concern for Emma's well-being by saying that he realizes how lousy his staring must make her feel. He could also try to understand what really bothers her about this behavior and reassure her that he does find her beautiful (maintaining focus on the problem at hand). He could ask her to point out when he slips into this pattern again so he can try to change his behavior: "I'm sorry. I do this out of habit, but I realize now that it's upsetting and disrespectful toward you. After all, I get upset when other men look at you even if you're not aware of it! I'll try to be more respectful, but if I lapse, I want you to call me on it."

Answer: Emma—Secure. Emma effectively communicates her needs. She tells Todd how his actions make her feel in a straight-forward, nonaccusatory manner (or as nonaccusatory as can be expected under the circumstances).

Secure tactics Emma could use: She did a good job.

6. Dan's sister comes to look after Dan and Shannon's kids while the two go out for some much needed time together. When they return, Shannon goes straight up to bed while Dan chats with his sister. Later Dan comes up to their room, fuming. "My sister is doing us a huge favor by babysitting, the least you could do is say hello to her!" In response Shannon says, "Did I really not even say hello? I'm so spaced out. I didn't mean to. I'm sorry."

Shannon's reaction is:
□ Secure
□ Insecure

Insecure tactics Shannon used:

_____

_____

Secure tactics Shannon could use:

_____

_____

Answer: Secure. Shannon avoids many insecure hazards. She refrains from generalizing the conflict. She doesn't react defensively and resort to counterattacks. She doesn't return tit for tat. She maintains focus on the problem at hand and responds to it and to it alone. This is not to say that Dan's anger will disappear; in fact, he most probably *will* remain irritated. But Shannon has managed to take the edge off his anger and avoid escalation. Her response shows that reacting securely to conflict is not rocket science; it doesn't require amazing verbal or psychological skills. It can often come down to simple but sincere apology.

Epilogue

For us, the most important take-home message from this book is that relationships should not be left to chance. Relationships are one of the most rewarding of human experiences, above and beyond other gifts that life has to offer. In fact, one study found that 73 percent of over three hundred university student participants were willing to sacrifice the majority of their goals in life for a romantic relationship. But despite the importance we assign to our most intimate bonds, most of us still know very little about the science behind romantic relationships and allow ourselves all too often to be guided by misconceptions and myths.

Even the two of us, having thoroughly studied the science behind adult attachment styles, occasionally find ourselves falling back into familiar patterns of thinking when we hear a certain love story or watch a romantic movie that pushes all our old buttons. We recently saw a popular boy-meets-girl film that did just that. A young man falls passionately in love with a beautiful and intelligent woman. He becomes consumed by the desire to spend the rest of his life with her. She, on the other hand, is determined to stay free and unattached—and tells him so from the start. Throughout the story, she sends mixed messages; she flirts and strings him along, which allows him to keep hoping for a happy ending. But in an atypical Hollywood twist, she breaks his heart. He later discovers that she has gone on to marry the man of her dreams and is living happily ever after. (Well, to the best of his, and our, knowledge, because the movie ends there.)

Our first reaction, along with the rest of the audience, was to fall in love with the woman. She was strong, passionate, independent—a truly free spirit. And she was honest; she warned him in advance that she wasn't looking for a serious relationship. We certainly couldn't fault her for that. Besides, he obviously just wasn't "the one" for her (after all, we were told she later found "the one"). For much of the movie we were also enthralled with the romantic possibility that she might open up to him and he would win her over. Although the film started with a spoiler—saying that it wasn't a love story—we never stopped wishing for its two stars to ride off into the sunset together.

But on second thought, we quickly realized we had bought into every possible relationship fallacy. Even we, with our professional understanding of the science behind romantic behavior, had reverted to our old—and very unhelpful—beliefs. We allowed some deeply ingrained misconceptions to influence our thinking.

The first misconception is that *everyone has the same capacity for intimacy.* We've been raised to believe that every person can fall deeply in love (this part might well be true) and that when this happens, he or she will be transformed into a different person (this part is not!). Regardless of what they were like before, when people find "the one," they supposedly become adoring, faithful, supportive partners—free of qualms about the relationship. It's tempting to forget that, in fact, *people have very different capacities for intimacy.* And when one person's need for closeness is met with another person's need for independence and distance, a lot of unhappiness ensues. By being cognizant of this fact, both of you can navigate your way better in the dating world to find someone with intimacy needs similar to your own (if you are unattached) or reach an entirely new understanding about your differing needs in an existing relationship—a first and necessary step toward steering it in a more secure direction.

The second common misconception we fell victim to is that *marriage is the be-all and end-all.* Romantic stories tend to end there, and we are all tempted to believe that when someone gets married, it's unequivocal proof of the power of love to transform; that the decision to marry means they're now ready for true closeness and emotional partnership. We don't like to admit that people might enter marriage without having these goals in mind, let alone the ability to achieve them. We want to believe, as we had hoped for in the movie, that once married, anyone can change and treat his/her spouse like royalty (especially if two people are deeply in love with each other).

In this book, however, we've shown how *mismatched attachment styles can lead to a great deal of unhappiness in marriage, even for people who love each other greatly.* If you are in such a relationship, don't feel guilty for feeling incomplete or unsatisfied. After all, your most basic needs often go unmet, and love alone isn't enough to make the relationship work. If you've read this book and understand where you are each coming from in terms of your attachment styles, you can now tackle this problem from a completely different angle.

Epilogue

The third hard-to-shed misconception we fell for is that *we alone are responsible for our emotional needs; they are not our partner's responsibility.* When potential partners "Mirandize" us and "read us our rights" (see chapter 11) early in a relationship by telling us that they aren't ready to commit, thereby renouncing responsibility for our well-being, or when they make unilateral decisions in a long-standing relationship without taking our needs into account, we're quick to accept these terms. This logic has become very natural to people, and our friends might say, "They told you in advance they didn't want to commit," or "They always said how strongly they feel about this issue, so you have no one but yourself to blame." But when we're in love and want to continue a relationship, we tend to ignore the contradictory messages we're getting. Instead of recognizing that someone who blatantly disregards our emotions is not going to be a good partner, we accept this attitude. Again, we must constantly remind ourselves: *In a* true *partnership,* both *partners view it as their responsibility to ensure the other's emotional well-being.*

Once we let go of these delusions, the movie, like many situations in life, takes on a very different meaning. The story line becomes predictable and loses much of its mystique. It's no longer a boy-meets-girl story, but an avoidant-meets-anxious one; he has a need for intimacy and she shies away from it. The writing was on the wall from the beginning, but the movie's male hero couldn't see it. That the woman he loved went on to marry someone else doesn't change the fact that she was avoidant, and it predicts nothing about her happiness (or her husband's) in the marriage. It's very likely that she continued her behavior and distanced herself from the husband in many ways. For all we know, the hero became her phantom ex.

What we learned from watching the film is just how hard it is to let go of concepts we've believed in our entire lives—no matter how unhelpful they've been. But jettisoning these ideas is a necessary step; holding on to them can be highly destructive. They encourage us to compromise our self-esteem and happiness by ignoring our most basic needs and trying to be someone we're not.

We believe that every person deserves to experience the benefits of a secure bond. When our partner acts as our secure base and emotional anchor, we derive strength and encouragement to go out into the world and make the most of ourselves. He or she is there to help us become the best person we can be, as we are for them.

Don't Lose Sight of These Facts:

- Your attachment needs are legitimate.
- You shouldn't feel bad for depending on the person you are closest to—it is part of your genetic makeup.
- A relationship, from an attachment perspective, should make you feel more self-confident and give you peace of mind. If it doesn't, this is a wake-up call!
- And above all, remain true to your authentic self—playing games will only distance you from your ultimate goal of finding true happiness, be it with your current partner or with someone else.

We hope you will use the relationship wisdom distilled in this book, from more than two decades of research, to find happiness

Epilogue

in your romantic connections and to soar in all aspects of your life. If you follow the attachment principles we have outlined, you will be actively giving yourself the best shot at finding—and keeping—a deeply gratifying love, instead of leaving one of the most important aspects of your life to chance!

ACKNOWLEDGMENTS

We are grateful to many people for helping us during the writing of this book. First and foremost, we thank our families for their support. We also extend a very special thanks to Nancy Doherty for her outstanding editorial work and unending encouragement. She is truly an exceptional person!

We're grateful to our agent, Stephanie Kip-Rostan, for her help and for introducing us to Sara Carder, our editor at Tarcher, who "got" the book when it was just an outline. Sara's insight and vision have been invaluable. We thank the entire Tarcher team for the great work they've done. In addition, we would like to give special thanks Eddie Sarfaty, Jezra Kaye, Jill Marsal, Giles Anderson, and Smriti Rao. Thanks to Ellen Landau and Lena Verdeli for their valuable comments on parts of the manuscript. Many thanks to Tziporah Kassachkoff, Donald Chesnut, Robert Risko, David Sherman, Jesse Short, Guy Kettelhack, Alexander Levin, Arielle Eckstut, Christopher Gustafson, Oren Tatcher, Dave Shamir, Amnon Yekutieli, Christopher Bergland, Don Summa,

Blanche Mackey, Leila Livingston, Michal Malachi Cohen, Adi Segal, and Margaret and Michael Korda. A special thanks to Dan Siegel, for his encouraging words about the manuscript and the important feedback he provided.

We want to acknowledge the volunteers who shared their intimate experiences and personal thoughts with us. We also thank those who took our Applied Adult Attachment questionnaires and gave us feedback on the beta version. Each and every person taught us something useful.

Writing this book would have been impossible without the rich legacy of innovative attachment research upon which we drew. We're forever indebted to the researchers who made groundbreaking discoveries in this field. They introduced us to a different—and ingenious—way of viewing relationships.

From Rachel

I thank the entire team at the Modiin Educational Psychology Service, where I have worked for the past four years. Their knowledge, insight, and collective wisdom have allowed me to become a better psychologist—as both a therapist and a diagnostician. Working in this supportive and rigorous setting allowed me to continue to learn and to expand my horizons on a daily basis.

I thank the Shinui Institute for Family and Marriage Therapy for introducing me to the systems perspective in psychotherapy, encouraging me to view and treat symptoms within the broadest possible context, taking into account the strong impact of our closest relationships on our lives. I also thank Batya Krieger, my first therapy supervisor, for her encouragement and guidance.

I extend special thanks to the people who influenced my thinking early in my career, including Dr. Harvey Hornstein, not only an outstanding professional and teacher but also an exceptionally generous person, and Dr. W. Warner Burke, for his wisdom and inspiration—both at Columbia University.

I express my gratitude to my parents: my father, Jonathan Frankel, who, to my dismay, didn't live to see this project come to fruition, and my mother, Edith Rogovin Frankel, who has helped in a multitude of ways. I am also grateful to my husband, Jonathan, for his love, support, friendship, and wisdom, and to my three children, who add depth and meaning to my life every single day.

From Amir

I've been fortunate to find an intellectual home for the past twelve years in the departments of psychiatry and neuroscience at Columbia University, where I've had the opportunity to work with superb clinicians and researchers. I am grateful to the many teachers, supervisors, mentors, and colleagues who've enriched my life and thinking. I specifically thank those who've had ongoing influence on my professional path: Dr. Rivka Eiferman at Hebrew University in Jerusalem, who taught me about the analytic attitude and how to reserve judgment when listening to patients; the late Dr. Jacob Arlow, whose work helped form the core of modern analytic thinking and from whom I was lucky enough to have learned psychotherapeutic practice; Dr. Lisa Mellman and Dr. Ron Rieder, who were instrumental in helping my development as a clinician and a researcher; Dr. Daniel Schechter, Principle Investigator in the Parent-Child Project at Columbia, who introduced me to attachment-based therapy with children and parents in the therapeutic nursery; Dr. Abby Fyer, from whom I learned a great deal in conversations over the years, and who taught me about the importance of the opioid system in attachment; Dr. Clarice Kestenbaum, for teaching me how to work with children and young adults in a very special way; and Dr. David Schaffer, who made my research career possible.

I also thank Dr. Dolores Malaspina, who taught me the basics of epidemiological research and the importance of community samples in medicine; Dr. Bill Byne, who discussed with me the literature on childhood gender nonconformity and taught me how to read scientific literature in a critical way; and Drs. Ann Dolinsky, David Leibow, and Michael Liebowitz, for the clinical teachings, knowledge, and experience they shared with me. Thanks to Dr. Rene Hen for his support through the years; to Dr. Myron Hofer, whose approach to studying development in animal models and whose work on the effects of early attachment on the adult phenotype are exemplary. I value his confidence in my work, and appreciate his guidance.

I would like to express my appreciation and admiration to my current collaborators, Dr. Eric Kandel, Dr. Denise Kandel, Dr. Samuel Schacher, and Dr. Claudia Schmauss. Working with them challenges my intellect and thinking in the best possible way.

Special thanks to the late Dr. Jimmy Schwartz, who gave me my first opportunity to perform neuroscience research; to Dr. Herb Kleber, for his open-door policy and illuminating discussions; to Dr. Francine Cournos, my first long-term therapy supervisor, for all the support she has given me over the years; and to all the friends and colleagues with whom I have been fortunate to work and from whose wisdom I have benefited.

I thank the National Institutes of Health for ongoing support of my research, which has contributed to the writing of this book.

I would like to express special gratitude to my family. Having them as a secure base gives me the courage to explore the world. And last but not least, I thank all my patients, children and adults alike, for sharing their struggles and hopes, frustration and dreams. Being a part of their lives has made me a better, richer person.

BIBLIOGRAPHY

Atkinson, L., A. Niccols, A. Paglia, J. Coolbear, K. C. H. Parker, L. Poulton, et al. "A Meta-Analysis of Time Between Maternal Sensitivity and Attachment Assessments: Implications for Internal Working Models in Infancy/Toddlerhood." *Journal of Social and Personal Relationships* 17 (2000): 791–810.

Baker, B., J. P. Szalai, M. Paquette, and S. Tobe. "Marital Support, Spousal Contact, and the Course of Mild Hypertension." *Journal of Psychosomatic Research* 55, no. 3 (September 2003): 229–33.

Brassard, A., P. R. Shaver, and Y. Lussier. "Attachment, Sexual Experience, and Sexual Pressure in Romantic Relationships: A Dyadic Approach." *Personal Relationships* 14 (2007): 475–94.

Brennan, K. A., C. L. Clark, and P. R. Shaver. "Self-Report Measurement of Adult Romantic Attachment: An Integrative Overview." In J. A. Simpson and W. S. Rholes, eds., *Attachment Theory and Close Relationships*. New York: Guilford Press, 1998, 46–76.

Cassidy, J., and P. R. Shaver. *Handbook of Attachment: Theory, Research, and Clinical Applications*. New York: Guilford Press, 1999.

Ceglian, C. P., and S. Gardner. "Attachment Style: A Risk for Multiple Marriages?" *Journal of Divorce and Remarriage* 31 (1999): 125–39.

Bibliography

Coan, J. A., H. S. Schaefer, and R. J. Davidson. "Lending a Hand: Social Regulation of the Neural Response to Threat." *Psychological Science* 17, no. 12 (2006): 1032–39.

Cohn, D. A., D. H. Silver, C. P. Cowan, P. A. Cowan, and J. Pearson. "Working Models of Childhood Attachment and Couple Relationships." *Journal of Family Issues* 13 (1992): 432–49.

Collins, N. L., and S. J. Read. "Adult Attachment, Working Models, and Relationship Quality in Dating Couples." *Journal of Personality and Social Psychology* 58 (1990): 644–63.

Creasey, G., and M. Hesson-McInnis. "Affective Responses, Cognitive Appraisals, and Conflict Tactics in Late Adolescent Romantic Relationships: Associations with Attachment Orientations." *Journal of Counseling Psychology* 48 (2001): 85–96.

———, K. Kershaw, and A. Boston. "Conflict Management with Friends and Romantic Partners: The Role of Attachment and Negative Mood Regulation Expectancies." *Journal of Youth and Adolescence* 28 (1999): 523–43.

Feeney, B. C. "A Secure Base: Responsive Support of Goal Strivings and Exploration in Adult Intimate Relationships." *Journal of Personality and Social Psychology* 87 (2004): 631–48.

———, and R. L. Thrush. "Relationship Influences on Exploration in Adulthood: The Characteristics and Functions of a Secure Base." *Journal of Personality and Social Psychology* 98, no. 1 (2010): 57–76.

Fraley, R. C., P. M. Niedenthal, M. J. Marks, C. C. Brumbaugh, and A. Vicary. "Adult Attachment and the Perception of Facial Expressions of Emotion: Probing the Hyperactivating Strategies Underlying Anxious Attachment." *Journal of Personality* 74 (2006): 1163–90.

———, N. G. Waller, and K. A. Brennan. "An Item Response Theory Analysis of Self-Report Measures of Adult Attachment." *Journal of Personality and Social Psychology* 78 (2000): 350–65.

Bibliography

George, C., N. Kaplan, and M. Main. "Adult Attachment Interview Protocol." Unpublished manuscript. University of California, Berkeley, 1984.

Gillath, O., S. A. Bunge, P. R. Shaver, C. Wendelken, and M. Mikulincer. "Attachment-Style Differences in the Ability to Suppress Negative Thoughts: Exploring the Neural Correlates." *NeuroImage* 28 (2005): 835–47.

Gillath, O., E. Selcuk, and P. R. Shaver. "Moving Toward a Secure Attachment Style: Can Repeated Security Priming Help?" *Social and Personality Psychology Compass* 2/4 (2008): 1651–66.

Gillath, O., P. R. Shaver, J. M. Baek, and S. D. Chun. "Genetic Correlates of Adult Attachment Style." *Personality and Social Psychology Bulletin*, 34 (2008): 1396–1405.

Gray, J. *Men Are from Mars, Women Are from Venus.* New York: HarperCollins, 1992.

Hammersla, J. F., and L. Frease-McMahan. "University Students' Priorities: Life Goals vs. Relationships." *Sex Roles: A Journal of Research* 23 (1990): 1–2.

Hazan, C., and P. R. Shaver. "Romantic Love Conceptualized as an Attachment Process." *Journal of Personality and Social Psychology* 52 (1987): 511–24.

———, D. Zeifman, and K. Middleton. "Adult Romantic Attachment, Affection, and Sex." Paper presented at the 7th International Conference on Personal Relationships, Groninger, The Netherlands, July 1994.

Johnson, S. *Attachment Processes in Couple and Family Therapy.* Susan M. Johnson, Ed.D., and Valerie E. Whiffen, Ph.D., eds. New York: Guilford Press, 2003.

Keelan, J. R., K. L. Dion, and K. K. Dion. "Attachment Style and Heterosexual Relationships Among Young Adults: A Short-Term Panel Study." *Journal of Social and Personal Relationships* 11 (1994): 141–60.

Bibliography

Kirkpatrick, L. A., and K. E. Davis. "Attachment Style, Gender, and Relationship Stability: A Longitudinal Analysis." *Journal of Personality and Social Psychology* 66 (1994): 502–12.

Krakauer, J. *Into the Wild.* New York: Anchor Books, 1997.

Main, M., and J. Solomon. "Discovery of a New, Insecure/Disorganized/Disoriented Attachment Pattern." In T. B. Brazelton and M. Yogman, eds., *Affective Development in Infancy,* pp. 95–124. Norwood, NJ: Ablex, 1986.

Mikulincer, M., V. Florian, and G. Hirschberger. "The Dynamic Interplay of Global, Relationship-Specific, and Contextual Representations of Attachment Security." Paper presented at the annual meeting of the Society for Personality and Social Psychology conference, Savannah, Ga., 2002.

———, and G. S. Goodman. *Dynamics of Romantic Love: Attachment, Caregiving, and Sex.* New York: Guilford Press, 2006.

———, and P. R. Shaver. *Attachment in Adulthood: Structure, Dynamics, and Change.* New York: Guilford Press, 2007.

Pietromonaco, P. R., and K. B. Carnelley. "Gender and Working Models of Attachment: Consequences for Perceptions of Self and Romantic Relationships." *Personal Relationships* 1 (1994): 63–82.

Rholes, W. S, and J. A. Simpson. *Adult Attachment: Theory, Research, and Clinical Implications.* New York: Guilford Press, 2004.

Schachner, D. A., and P. R. Shaver. "Attachment Style and Human Mate Poaching." *New Review of Social Psychology* 1 (2002): 122–29.

Shaver, P. R., and M. Mikulincer. "Attachment-Related Psychodynamics." *Attachment and Human Development* 4 (2000): 133–61.

Siegel, D. J. *The Developing Mind: How Relationships and the Brain Interact to Shape Who We Are.* New York: The Guilford Press, 2001.

Bibliography

————. *Mindsight: The New Science of Personal Transformation.* New York: Bantam, 2010.

————. *Parenting from the Inside Out: How a Deeper Self-Understanding Can Help You Raise Children Who Thrive.* New York: Tarcher/Penguin, 2003.

Simpson, J. A. "Influence of Attachment Styles on Romantic Relationships." *Journal of Personality and Social Psychology* 59 (1990): 971–80.

Simpson, J. A., W. Ickes, and T. Blackstone. "When the Head Protects the Heart: Empathic Accuracy in Dating Relationships." *Journal of Personality and Social Psychology* 69: 629–41.

————, W. S. Rholes, L. Campbell, and C. L. Wilson. "Changes in Attachment Orientations Across the Transitions to Parenthood." *Journal of Experimental Social Psychology* 39 (2003): 317–31.

Strickland, B. B. *The Gale Encyclopedia of Psychology.* Michigan: Gale Group, 2007.

Watson, J. B. *Psychological Care of Infant and Child.* New York: W. W. Norton Company, Inc., 1928.

INDEX

Index

Index

Index

Index

parent-child bonding, 7, 21–25,
    138–39, 145
physiological unity, 27–28
secure style's expectations of, 144
"still waters run deep," 93

male stereotypes, 54, 55, 107–8
manipulation, 58
    as protest behavior, 87
marriage, 56
    fear of, 53, 67–68
    loneliness in, 3–4
    misconception about, 270–71
Marsha and Craig story, 196–202
    as opposing forces, 202–3
    rebound effect, 209–10
    relentless/never-ending deactivating
        strategies, 205–6
masochistic borderline personality traits,
    78, 82
McCandles, Chris, 109–12
memories, after breakup, 214
Men Are From Mars, Women Are From Venus,
    122–23
mental flexibility, secure attachment style's,
    55, 136–37
Mikulincer, Mario, 89, 120–21, 145, 147
Miranda's Law of Dating, 117, 237–38, 271
mixed messages, 4–7, 100
"morph movie" technique, 79–80
mother-child bonding, 7–8, 21–25, 138–39
    secure mother's, 145

"neediness," as fault, 52
needs, 56, 100
    communicating your needs, 231–33
    feels incomplete on own, 70, 73–74,
        270–71
    focus on your, 235
    responsiveness to, 142–43
New School of Psychology, Israel, 120–21
Niedenthal, Paula, 79–80
nine strategies, for surviving breakup,
    213–15
non-interference, 141

off-limits topics, 54
"the one," who is never you, 53, 125–26,
    129, 269–70

origins, of attachment, 47–48
oxytocin, 251–52

pampering, after breakup, 214
parent-child bonding, 7, 21–25, 138–39
    secure mother's, 145
parent-child pairs, 138–39
partner's attachment style, 49–51
    cheat sheet for deciphering, 65–66
    Golden Rules for deciphering, 62–65
    questionnaire: Group A, 52–54
    questionnaire: Group B, 55–57
    questionnaire: Group C, 57–59
pets, as inspiration, 165
phantom ex, 124–25, 129
Phillips, Suzanne, 165
physical affection, 22, 57
    avoiding, 117
    "cuddle hormone," 251–52
    secure person's, 136–37
    universal need for closeness, 113
physiological unity, 27–28
Pietromonaco, Paul, 91
plans together
    left unclear, 53
    reliable and consistent, 55
    vacations, 53, 57
    your preferences honored, 55
positive conflict-resolution tactics, 253
positive outlook, secure attachment style's,
    136–37
prevention, of conflict, 251–52
principles
    conflict busting, 245
    of effective communication, 235–37
    insecure people's difficulty with secure
        resolution principles, 252–53
    secure, for making conflict work,
        245–51
promises, kept, 55
protest behavior, 12, 106
    in digital age, 14–15
    typical, 86–88
Psychological Care of Infant and Child
    (Watson), 22

questionnaire
    attachment style, 40–43
    partner's attachment style, 51–59

289

Index

Index

ABOUT THE AUTHOR

Dr. Amir Levine, who grew up in Israel and Canada, has always had a fascination with biology and the brain. His mother, a popular science editor who valued creativity and self-motivation, allowed him to stay home from school whenever he wanted and study what interested him. Although this freedom sometimes got him into trouble, during high school he wrote his first large-scale work, about birds of prey in the Bible and in ancient Assyria and Babylon. His thesis examined the evolution of symbolism from a culture of multiple deities to one of monotheism. After high school, Levine served as a press liaison in the Israeli army. He worked with renowned journalists such as Thomas Friedman, Glenn Frankel, and Ted Koppel, and was awarded a citation of excellence.

After his compulsory army service, having developed a passion for working with people as well as a love for science, Levine enrolled in medical school at Hebrew University in Jerusalem, where he received numerous awards. During medical school, he organized student meetings with Dr. Eiferman, a psychoanalyst, to discuss

About the Author

how doctors can preserve their sensitivity to the hospitalized patients' needs while negotiating a complex hospital hierarchy. He was awarded the faculty prize for his graduation thesis, "Human Sexuality Viewed from the Perspective of Childhood Gender Nonconformity," which was later adapted for a university seminar.

Levine's interest in human behavior led him to a residency in adult psychiatry at New York Presbyterian Hospital/Columbia University/New York State Psychiatric Institute, where he was ranked first in his class for three consecutive years. He received several awards, including an American Psychoanalytic Fellowship, which gave him a rare opportunity to work with a world-renowned psychoanalyst, the late Jacob Arlow. Levine then specialized in child and adolescent psychiatry. While working in a therapeutic nursery with mothers with posttraumatic stress disorder and their toddlers, he witnessed the power of attachment to heal and realized the importance of attachment principles in the daily lives of adults as well as children. During the last year of his three-year fellowship, he joined the lab of the late James (Jimmy) Schwartz, a renowned neuroscientist.

Currently at Columbia University, Levine is a principle investigator, together with Nobel Prize laureate Dr. Eric Kandel and distinguished researcher Dr. Denise Kandel, on a research project sponsored by the National Institutes of Health. He also has a private practice in Manhattan.

Levine is board-certified in adult psychiatry and is a member of the American Psychiatric Association, the American Academy of Child and Adolescent Psychiatry, and the Society for Neuroscience.

He lives with his family in New York City and Southampton, New York.

About the Author

. . .

For as long as she can remember, Rachel Heller has been interested in human behavior and culture. As the daughter of two university professors—a historian and a political scientist—she spent her childhood in the United States, England, Israel, and other countries. Perhaps as a result of this early experience and her keen interest in diverse cultures, she became an avid traveler, spending long periods of time in, among other countries, India, Indonesia, the Philippines, Uganda, Kenya, Madagascar, and Pakistan, where she trekked in the high Himalayas and learned about local traditions, hiking, and exploring.

Before entering the field of psychology, Heller worked as a tour guide for American, British, Australian, and South African volunteers in the Israeli army as part of her compulsory army service. Later she served as an aide to a member of the Israeli Knesset, conducting research on legislation and working with the press, especially on human rights issues.

Heller holds a B.A. in behavioral sciences (psychology, anthropology, and sociology) and an M.A. degree in social-organizational psychology from Columbia University. After completing her master's, she worked for several management consulting firms, including PricewaterhouseCoopers, KPMG, and Towers Perrin, where she managed high-profile clients.

Before a recent move to the San Francisco Bay Area, where she now lives with her husband and three children, Heller worked for the Educational Psychology Service in Modi'in. There she helped families, couples, and children within various educational settings to improve their relationships and lives.